An Atheist Haggadah for Zionists

elias lightstone

Published by elias lightstone, 2024.

AN ATHEIST HAGGADAH FOR ZIONISTS

First edition. April 15, 2024.

ISBN: 979-8224920839

Written by elias lightstone.

for the dead who show us the future and the living who can see the past.

INTRODUCTION

People turn to religion for many reasons: Fear of death, comfort in bad times, community and fellowship, need for a leader...

I find my solace for these issues elsewhere.

This is my version of the Passover Haggadah, created when I could no longer in good faith, (pardon the expression), participate in the traditional service that I have attended in one form or another every year for more than 70 years with head bowed and opinions safely left elsewhere.

For me, beliefs must be supported by verifiable evidence, otherwise they are simply desperate inventions the mind can only pretend to.

There are Christian preachers who have said (I have heard this directly from the horse's mouth) that Adolf Eichmann had a better chance of getting into heaven than any of his victims *"if he took Jesus into his heart before he died. Good deeds won't get you into heaven, only faith in Jesus."*

This kind of fanatical, and outright despicable statement should disgust anybody; but it is a genuinely held belief and the kind of thinking that informs everything around it.

Once you fall under the spell of this idea, you become a manipulated fool who believes whatever the priest tells you. You drink the kool-aid on command, *a le* Jim Jones – either literally or metaphorically.

These people carry on protracted "serious" discussions about whether cremated individuals will get "raptured" when the time comes.

For the Jews it's a little more complicated (but no less idiotic) because "our god" is not an actual corporeal being, and is not "...a personal God quaquaquaqua,..."(1) but we all wait for him, nonetheless. The consequences of this are de facto salvation. In other words, if the messiah arrived there wouldn't be anything to discuss; that would be the end of the world as we know it and the beginning of heaven on earth. Or something like that. Only praying almost incessantly over just about everything can hasten the "Coming."

Here is 'God' in his own words (according to the Pirkei Avot, in English (Ethics of the Fathers):

As is stated (Isaiah 43:7)[1]**: "All that is called by My name and for My glory, I created it, formed it, also I made it."**

On the face of it, he seems to be a self-glorifying psychopath.

I have my own hypothesis:

Once upon a time there was 'God' and there was 'Satan', and they fought a mighty battle for control of the universe.

God lost and the world was born.

1. https://www.chabad.org/15974#v7

It makes perfect sense that Satan would create a civilization of slaves to worship him while he sits up there stirring the pot and laughing.

<u>The greatest trick the devil ever pulled, was to turn people into believers.</u>

Being fair, there is also truth and wisdom in the old writings that should not be thrown out with the bath water, so to speak.

For example: (Republicans take note)

> ***Rabbi Chanina, deputy to the kohanim, would say: "Pray for the integrity of the government; for were it not for the fear of its authority, a man would swallow his neighbor alive."***

But it doesn't take long for the usual nonsense to take over.

> ***Rabbi Yaakov would say: One who walks along a road and studies, and interrupts his studying to say, "How beautiful is this tree!", "How beautiful is this ploughed field!"—-the Torah considers it as if he had forfeited his life.***

> ***Or this:***

> ***On March 1, 2024 The Jerusalem Post reported that two serving IDF soldiers were sent to prison***

> ***for twenty days for making hot dogs in a kosher kitchen on a Saturday.*** *(https://www.jpost.com/omg/article-789809)*

There are so many examples of material like this it isn't worth reciting. I'm picking on Christians and Jews, but systemic lunacy is part of the substructure of every religion, and it wouldn't take ten minutes to unearth equally nonsensical assertions from any cult in the human lexicon.

There is no such thing as mainstream religion. They are all cults, and they are all pervasively evil and can take responsibility for the most gruesome, horrifying events in human history.

But don't take my word for it; you have all the world's knowledge at your fingertips; of course, you will have to be prepared to accept evidence rather than fancy.

Be that as it may, you will find in this pamphlet some of the traditional rituals, commentary, and ideas from the original seder observed by Jews for the last 3,000 years.

For the second part, I hold an unwavering commitment to Zionism.

Over the years I became concerned with the direction Israel seemed to be going vis a vis the neighboring populations and most recently, the cynical attempt by the Netanyahu government to end the judicial oversight of parliament.

When I say concerned, I mean I feared anything that might be used as more ammunition to defame the country and the Zionist ideal in the eyes of the world, a problem exacerbated almost daily by United Nations Jew-baiting and Palestinian lies which, for some reason are taken at face value by governments, news organizations, movie stars, circus clowns and anyone else with a 'Jewish problem.'

Palestinians who are in fact Jordanians despised by other Jordanians who bar them from entering their country, (Jordan murdered 25,000 of their erstwhile fellow citizens not so long ago) are to a considerable extent the authors of their own misfortune having turned down several opportunities for statehood because what they want is Israel itself, *judenrein.*

That is precisely and exactly what the phrase 'from the river to the sea,' means.

From Associated Press:

> King Abdullah II gave a message on
> Tuesday, Oct. 17, 2023, saying:
> **"No refugees in Jordan,**
> **no refugees in Egypt."**

Notwithstanding the Yom Kippur surprise attack in 1973 and an endless litany of terrorist murders over the years, Jew-hatred as understood by us, and our parent's generation was a thing of the past. Unfriendly remarks, contemptable, appalling public statements, juvenile anti-Semitism, brain-dead left-wing university professors, pockets of neo-Nazis, laughable idiocy from the left in general, while none of it pleasant, did not appear existentially threatening. After Hitler and Auschwitz, Einsatzgruppen, and Lodz, Stalingrad, Babi Yar, what more could they do?

People have a right to hate, and where is it written you gotta like Jews?

But on October 7, 2023, any illusions about the gentile world were shattered into the million glittering pieces of *Kristallnacht redux.*

Hillel's famous quote: ***"If I am not for myself, who will be for me, and if not now, when?"*** is what must be taken from this attack and the appalling, disgusting, reprehensible response of the world.

This Passover Haggadah is meant to be a living document, cognizant of the fact that:

"Governments... (or traditions) ... long established should not be changed for light and transient Causes; and accordingly, all Experience hath shewn, that Mankind are more disposed to suffer, while Evils are sufferable, than to right themselves by abolishing the Forms to which they are accustomed."

(American Declaration of Independence)

October 7, 2023, was not light or transient and it calls for a profound reassessment of our place in the world. Many have pointed out that if Jews are not safe in Israel, there is nowhere left to go, something the Jewish *ideocracy* of the left can't seem to grasp.

They are marching right along with their "friends and neighbors" clamoring for Jewish blood and dancing in the streets calling for a final solution to the Jewish problem, for the destruction of the country and the scattering of the tribes once again.

As the times around us change, as putative allies suddenly join us at the barricades, or invite us to their cause (invariably for temporary and pragmatic reasons) we must be aware, we must realize that we are always on our own, regardless of how sincere any particular courtship appears to be in the moment.

> *The National Association for the Advancement of Colored People (NAACP) was founded in part by Jews. Jews marched with Martin Luther King. In 1964, Andrew Goodman and Michael Schwerner, two Jewish civil rights workers went to Mississippi to register black voters during a period of practiced, legal apartheid. They were murdered by the Ku Klux Klan.*
>
> *Today black Americans count themselves among the most anti-Semitic groups in the United States, led by Black Lives Matter (BLM). And let's not forget*

Lewis Farrakhan, the pre-eminent black racist in the country.

Jews who forget this evolve into anti-Semitic/Israel fraternities such as Students for Justice in Palestine, Palestinian Youth Movement, U.S. Palestinian Community Network, Within Our Lifetime, United for Palestine, Jewish Voice for Peace, If Not Now, and the Party for Socialism and Liberation, certainly among the most recognizable and repulsive organizations to ever take up the Jew-hate banner. Infamous professional Jewish anti-Semites who shall remain unnamed here but are well known, defend, befriend and cultivate them as they shill for each other. It is from among these types, the death camp kapos, the Jewish ghetto police, the informers and the traitors were culled.

But something else must be acknowledged regarding these deluded, self-haters: They look at what is happening in Israel and are justifiably horrified.

This is not who I am, this not what it means to be a Jew and if it does, I don't want to be one.

(I hate to break it to you, but you don't get to decide if you are a Jew or not a Jew and it has nothing whatsoever to do with your mother; the decision is in the hands of your enemies. You can claim to be anything you want, but you will die as a Jew.)

The civilian deaths that Hamas is responsible for that taint the IDF, and the country are truly horrifying, and no one would want to be associated with tragedies of this magnitude - even those who have sponsored them and try to deny culpability.

The responsible parties in this case are all who have enabled and coddled Hamas, including: The United Nations, above all and various European governments, Universities around the world, Doctors Without Borders, Church groups world-wide, NGOs, The Red Cross, which provides the necessary documents so convicted terrorists can get paid while they are in prison, Amnesty International and many more.

They believe and propagate the lies, have poured billions into the personal fortunes of the Hamas leadership and cheered as they murdered and raped their way through southern Israel.

The leadership of Hamas has stolen more than 11 billion dollars from the development funds sent to Gaza, socking it away in Swiss bank accounts and living lives of stunning luxury in Qatar while sending the dupes in Gaza out to die for the cause.

ABU MARZUK 3 BILLION
KHALED MASHAL 4 BILLION
ISMAIL HANIYEH 4 BILLION

Every NGO, every government on earth and most certainly the quasi-criminal enterprise a.k.a. the U.N. is fully aware, yet they continue to send billions to Hamas. Eleven billion dollars buys a lot of sewers, water systems, electricity and food. If people are starving in Gaza it is because Hamas wants them to starve. Hamas knows how the world will react and so do we.

There is not another cause or issue in memory (with the exception of the world wars and possibly the American intervention in Vietnam) that has gathered such a widespread group of people willing to march in step across faiths, international boundaries, political systems, race and gender. Not Bosnia, 100,000 dead; Guatemala, 170,000 dead; the Ustase, a pro-Nazi group that murdered Jews and Serbs and boiled people alive, 100,000 to 700,000 (actual count unknown); murder of Greeks by the Turks (10,000); Armenia, 1.5 million; Biafra 2 million; 180,000 Kurds murdered by Saddam Hussein; oh, I almost forgot: Six million Jews murdered by the Germans.

Now, all that was "olden times."

YEAR	DEATHS	ENTITY	PROTESTS
1971	3 million	Bangladesh	NONE
1979	3 million	Cambodia	NONE
1980s	300,000	Zimbabwe	NONE
1980s	160,000	Guatemala	NONE
1987	200,000	Somalia	NONE
1994	800,000	Rwanda	NONE
2002	70,000	Congo	NONE
2003	500,000	Darfur	NONE
2008	40,000	Sri Lanka	NONE
2009	55,000	Chechen	NONE
2014	18,000	Iraq	NONE
2015	580,000	Syria	NONE
2016	40,000	Rohingya	NONE
2016	383,000	South Sudan	NONE
2017	377,000	Yemen	NONE
2022	800,000	Ethiopia	NONE

Millions have been murdered in actual, real, premeditated, genocidal campaigns, a number of them ongoing at this moment.

There appears to be no evidence such as news stories of anyone, anywhere, doing any protesting (other than the victims, themselves, of course). Surely there must be a professional protest imbecile with a little leftover juice who could spare a few minutes.(!) I would bet these individuals marching and rioting around campuses and cities, desecrating graves, clogging the roads, terrifying the elderly, ripping down posters, mocking Holocaust survivors, threatening nursery schools and temples, praising Hamas and Bin Laden don't even recognize the names listed here.

Do they know where the countries are located, what continents are referred to, what actually happened, and why?

The answer to all is, NO.

It wasn't about Israel and Jews, so it didn't interest them.

Even natural enemies "Queers" *(their term for themselves)* and Muslims join forces against the evil Jew, until of course the Muslims kick them out of the club – for being "queer." The fact that "queers" are routinely murdered in every Islamic country on earth but are protected and live as freely in Israel as in the United States is totally lost on them. This is dismissed as something called "pink washing," in other words a ploy to divert attention from the "Palestinian genocide."

The Jerusalem Post, Feb. 8, 2024:

"A court of the Iranian-backed Houthis in Yemen has sentenced 13 people to public execution on homosexuality charges, ***the French wire service AFP reported***[1] *(arguably one of the most anti-Israel/anti-Semitic news organizations in the word) on Tuesday. Another 35 people have been detained for similar charges."*

It wasn't about Israel and Jews, so it didn't interest them.

A new campaign launched a website to raise awareness about the Hamas terrorist movement's lethal actions targeting the persecuted LGBTQ+ community in the Gaza[2] Strip.

The Equality Campaign Inc. created a website called "Queer in Gaza: The Reality" that states "Learn the Facts about Hamas' treatment of LGBT Palestinians."

The website declares "Living as a Queer person in Gaza is punishable by torture and death by

1. https://today.lorientlejour.com/article/1367225/13-sentenced-to-death-for-homosexuality-in-yemen-source.html

2. https://www.jpost.com/j-spot/article-771739

> Hamas, the rulers of Gaza" and "There is no transgender population in Gaza because any trans person who lives openly will be hunted down by Hamas." (Jerusalem Post March 7, 2024).

It makes no difference whatsoever to the west's "Queers for Palestine."

They will continue to March in support of Hamas.

The LGBTQ folks in America, England, Australia, etc., have not even registered this information never mind addressed it.

Tel Aviv is the largest (and one of the only) Pride celebrations in the Middle East... and it also happens to be considered* one of the largest in the world. *Tel Aviv doesn't have a specific "gayborhood", but instead, is incredibly LGBTIQ-friendly throughout. In fact, the Boston Globe cites Tel Aviv as having 25% of its population identify as gay, literally making it one of the gayest places on Earth.

(https://www.lonelyplanet.com/articles/most-gay-friendly-countries)

more information: https://www.equaldex.com/region/israel

Hating Israel is so important to these cretins that they would rather be thrown off a ten-story building (literally) or strangled at the end of a crane in the center of the city, buried alive, stoned to death or beheaded than even remain on the sidelines of this fight, never mind joining the side of the Jews.

That is who these people are. They are the most pathological Jew-haters on the planet after committed Nazis, and their ranks are filled with Jewish "queers" who proclaim this ideology, believing this will somehow make "normal" society find them acceptable.

Many patriotic, learned Jews of note from religious scholars to former IDF soldiers have criticized Israel's post-1967 political and social dynamic almost from the moment the Six Day War ended. There is a not inconsiderable number of Israelis who abhor the current situation and are active, vehement critics of the government, (along with a number of Arab, Muslim members of Israeli's *apartheid* Knesset) and call daily for a solution – but very few call for the dissolution of the country.

These protesters in America, Canada, Britain, Australia, France to name a few notwithstanding their monumental, deliberate, self-induced ignorance and their urge to join crowds in a kind of political rave are also motivated by an important characteristic necessary for the salvation of humanity and the solution to the "Palestinian problem" – compassion; but theirs is a mindless, untutored, florid compassion spurting from the belief that bad should not exist; all *bads* are of equal magnitude no matter what; knowledge, facts or evidence are overrated and as racist as geometry and don't matter at all if you believe something with all your heart; brown and black always trump white and most important: all bad can be eliminated ***if we could just get rid of the Jews.***

The worst of these groups are the Jews themselves. They do not admit that they hate being Jews in the case of organizations like JVP or they just hate Jews, period as in the case of the so-called socialists and so-called 'Social Justice Warriors' who are primarily, ignorant, imbecilic, dedicated "useful idiots," being manipulated by Qatar whose billions have bought stooges in every western country.

The bedrock of their apostasy is their belief that Jewish behavior creates anti-Semitism, that Jews have it coming, that the Jews deserve everything they get.

They do not understand or can't believe how deeply rooted and autonomic Jew-hate is. A stunning instance of this - by no means the worst, but a flagrant histrionic example - was the public statements by the actor, Susan Sarandon who attended one of these hate-fests and declared that Jews in the United States who were intimidated because of the surge in anti-Semitism should take note:

"There are a lot of people that are afraid, that are afraid of being Jewish at this time, and are getting a taste of what

it feels like to be a Muslim in this country [the USA], so often subjected to violence."

The statement is so telling that you wonder if the woman is really as densely stupid and ignorant as she sounds or if she's just being provocative. She made this statement when Jews were running from street attacks, bomb threats at synagogues, mobs swarming nursery schools and death threats from every side – much of it from her pet Muslims. To tell Jews they need to learn what it is like to be afraid after what has happened in the last, let's say 3000 years shows an ignorance or a malice beyond belief.

It is pure malice. She will deny this because there may yet be consequences in this society for that kind of utterance, but no apology can erase the fact that her first impulse was to jump up and start screaming, *'Jews are afraid? Good! About damn time.'*

She did issue a blubbering, obsequious apology with all the usual cliches and canned platitudes about "wording" and "phrasing," "I didn't mean it, please feel sorry for me..." after her remarks cost her professional representation (No doubt Jews were behind her ouster) and in the same breath vowed to be back at another hate-fest screaming about Israeli apartheid, colonialism, occupation, dead babies, Muslim family love and of course the new word of the week: genocide, at the first opportunity.

This is the kind of individual influencing generations that believe movie stars, basketball players, country singers and "gangstas" are not empty, studio puppets but actually the characters they portray. A basketball player says he thinks the world is flat: *So-and-so is famous that's good enough for me.*

I cannot reprint two articles on this subject. There isn't space and it's not considered fair use of another's work. But I can provide internet links.(2)

Possessing an attention span measured in seconds and minutes, no judgment, no curiosity, no desire for truth they respond only to something they can believe in, the more dramatic the better – after all, faith is more important than facts. Facts, like mathematics are racist. Facts are confusing because they don't fit into the fantasy. Facts are no use when it comes to creating chaos and mayhem.

It might be funny or simply pathetic, but these people can vote, and their numbers are growing while useless, stupid, incompetent baby boomers and their parents whose efforts basically created this society - all of it from Polio vaccines to and including global warming - are dying off.

An entire generation of people are coming out of universities like Harvard who have been both politically indoctrinated and fundamentally de-educated when it comes to critical thinking. Fold in AI, Facebook, Twitter, X...

The universities aided and abetted this because it suits a political agenda to flip the west upside down as they giggle gleefully from the sidelines and pursue the *triumph of their will.*

Focus on the Jews and people will flock to your cause.

The majority of Jews have not yet drunk the WOKE Kool-Aid, and this has created a minor problem for Harvard, this giant ($50-billion-dollar juggernaut) in terms of donations and reputation.

But nothing is going to end Harvard's control or dominance in education.

The incredible United States Congressional testimony December 5th, 2023, about campus anti-Semitism was profound in the way it mirrored the claims of Adolf Eichmann at his trial, where he described mass murder as merely a logistics problem, devoid of any human component.

For Claudine Gay (president of Harvard University at the time), screaming 'kill the Jews,' is technically not a threat concordant with the checklist provided by the school government that sets standards. According to Gay and the governing board of directors and their lawyers, one supposes you must actually start killing Jews before Harvard University will intervene.

In her subsequent abhorrent, self-serving, hypocritical "apology" after enormous public pressure, she blubbered "Words matter."

"It makes me sad," she declared, and face graven with theatrical contrition, she looked *sadly* at the floor. It was grotesque, clownish staging to quiet the critics. It seemed truly sociopathic; someone who can imitate what she thinks is empathy, she just doesn't have any. She wants sympathy!

Imagine if a student organization called Friends of the KKK marched around campus with a burning cross and noose shouting "Kill the n———," what would have happened?

Would this contravene Harvard's rules on hate speech and harassment?

Would this be protected speech?

Would the group actually have to lynch a black student to get Gay's attention?

Would she call in law enforcement to surround and protect the free speech and right of assembly due these noble protestors?

Within hours of her admittedly disastrous testimony, Jews on Harvard's campus invited her to light the school's Hanukkah menorah and there are pictures of her laughing and smiling, her Jewish accomplices surrounding her in a warm cloak of welcome.

You could almost hear the death camp commander telling the Jewish secretaries dutifully recording the murder statistics***, don't worry, you'll be the last to be gassed.***

Some of Nazism's earliest and most vocal support came from the universities (among many eager acolytes) and spread outward from there, and Harvard University was at the forefront of American efforts to legitimize Nazism and 'sell' it to the American people, including alliances with the most anti-Semitic universities in Germany where students and teachers danced in the firelight of burning Jewish books, and of course, eventually burning Jews, period. (3)

Finally forced to resign following an avalanche of allegations of serial plagiarism going back decades, she decried her resignation was orchestrated by racists as did the talking heads, commentators and news organizations genuflecting before their left-wing overlords and as could be expected within days, the word 'racists' was replaced with the word, 'Jews,' by all the usual suspects.

Even if this is true and Jews were behind her ouster (and certainly there were quite a few applying pressure) the real important part of the story is this:

Jews who defend themselves create anti-Semitism!

You can say whatever they want about Jews, but Jews are not permitted to reply or defend themselves because obviously if they are being attacked the disparagement must be justified – why else would people attack them?

She got to keep her nearly 1-million-dollar a year salary and was sent back to the classroom to pour her skills and knowledge - well, they might not even really be hers! - down the throats of her acolytes.

In response to the accusations of Harvard's indifference to Jewish students with their obvious and justifiable fears, the university decided to create a task force to "investigate" anti-Semitism and appointed faculty member Derek Penslar, as co-chairman.

Penslar signed a letter (along with a few thousand others) that includes this statement: "*...the direct link between Israel's recent attack on the judiciary and its illegal occupation*[3] *of millions of Palestinians in the Occupied Palestinian Territories.*"

---

3. *https://www.un.org/unispal/document/auto-insert-178619/*

In his book, Zionism: An Emotional State, he writes: *"Jewish culture was steeped in fantasies and occasionally, acts of vengeance against Christians." (4)*

Does anyone really believe the congressional investigation of Harvard or Harvard's investigation of itself is going to have any effect on anything?

Gay, and the governing board of Harvard are merely the latest iterations of an old theme, salted with DEI, Black Lives Matter, gender pronoun insanity and the over-arching oppression of Halloween costumes (Yale, I know)

In typical style this information will be soon lost under successive waves of scandals, fake news, canned reportage and probably natural disasters relevant to the moment. Succeeding generations should know this, and it should be recounted on the 15th day of Nisan, every year and amended accordingly until such time as a generation comes to ***know***, not merely ***believe*** it is no longer relevant.

Much good has come from the old, eastern-European societies, despite religion and truthfully, much has come *because* of it. The imperative to read and think and dispute has created a body of thought and literature (and in the evolutionary sense a selected trait to pass on), that propelled the 'people' to a position of prominence that has earned them disproportionate success and disproportionate, inexplicable grief.

(1) From Samuel Beckett's Waiting for Godot

(2) **https://www.cbssports.com/nba/news/kyrie-irving-apologizes-for-saying-earth-is-flat-claims-he-was-into-conspiracies/**

(2) https://www.newsweek.com/shaquille-oneal-earth-flat-explanation-podcast-1736414

(3) I direct your attention to this website: **https://www.jstor.org/stable/23887353**, and the work of Stephen H. Norwood.
(4) ***https://slate.com/news-and-politics/2024/01/*** *derek-penslar-harvard-jewish-antisemitism-task-force-israel.html)*

HAGGADAH

READER: Tonight, this 15th day of the Hebrew month of Nisan is the first night of Passover, where we assemble in remembrance of our ancestors' delivery from slavery in the land of Egypt 3000 years ago but more truly to acknowledge that this condition we so cherish is chimerical and turns to dust the moment it is within our grasp.

How often have we buried the bones and spirit of Amalek only to see him reborn anew with sharpened tooth and eyes of blood?

For it is written that ***"in every generation they rise against us."***

And so, begins this Passover Seder (and like all the others before it), a duet of hope and sorrow, each eclipsing the other in turn as the times may direct.

Typically, we say: ***"All who are hungry, come and eat; all who are in need join us for Passover."***

But we say that here with a caveat, for it is no longer our part to invite all to join our table in the belief they will reciprocate our offer of friendship. We have extended a hand to many oppressed groups, seeing in them ourselves and offering our understanding and sympathy and often our very lives in their cause only to be rebuked as they fall into the orbit of our enemies and turn on us with eyes of radiant hatred.

Join us if you want to know who we are; soon enough we will find out who you are, and you will be judged accordingly. Now we ask, are you with *us?* and those who claim to stand aside in some all-embracing neutrality will be seen as among those who stand against us.

If you cannot declare yourself an ally, this table is not for you.

Neither, in this seder do we supplicate ourselves before a mysterious, hidden deity. We shall not sing its praises nor beg forgiveness for alleged and imagined trespasses. If such a force and being exists, let it present itself and be recognized.

ALL: We set aside this glass of wine and implore this god to join us, and we ask: "If not now, when?"

For 3000 years the answer has been silence.

And yet still, we shall bless the candles, we shall bless the wine, we shall bless the bread in humble acknowledgment that the universe is unknown and mostly unknowable, and the natural miracles of bread and wine and light sustain us and are priceless gifts.

ALL:

- We are in awe of the atom and the photon and their union that created it all, including ourselves.
- We are grateful for consciousness and the ability to see and create and understand.
- We are grateful to be here, to contemplate the beautifully impossible notion of life itself and our ability to recognize it.
- We are humbled by the fact that here we sit while others suffer unimaginably, and it is nothing more than simple luck that placed us here and we claim no credit or virtue or special status for our good fortune. ***Rabbi Levitas of Yavneh would say: 'Be very, very humble, for the hope of mortal man is worms.'***
- Even though we may have worked and striven for our meager successes and accomplishments and gain, we acknowledge that it is a great gift of the universe to even be able to do so and nothing we have earned do we deserve more than does he who sleeps away his summers and weeps in the bitter winter night. ***Rabbi Yannai would say: 'We have no comprehension of the tranquility of the wicked, nor of the suffering of the righteous.'***
- We wish no man ill who treats us in kind; but neither will we suffer undeserved opprobrium. ***"For to those who honor me, I accord honor; those who scorn me shall be demeaned."***
- We shall stand by each other in just cause remembering that justice is an ephemeral maiden who adheres to whoever claims her and is quickly

turned to another without a backwards glance.

- If truth is a construction of facts as easily fitted to an unjust cause as a just one, truth must be looked upon with a cool and critical gaze, even to one's own detriment.
- We seek only our place in the world, an infinitesimal drop in the ocean of humanity, and seek no ascendence over any group or caste but claim the right of every man and woman to influence the circumstances of our lives by means agreed to among the parties.

READER: But our inordinate success in life is routinely discredited as fraud and we are imbued with occult powers, evil propensities and a tribal chauvinism that supernaturally disadvantages our competitors and enleagues us with the phantom wraith, Satan.

We ask ourselves, **"what have we done but succeed?"**

No admission, no correction, no appeal yields an answer yet the electric current of Jew-hate races through crowds igniting hysterical lethality among those who have never set eyes upon one who calls himself a Jew, yet their forked tongues burn with accusations unedited by fact, spewing forth as though they had witnessed these alleged crimes firsthand.

No god has ever swept the lies and contumely from the minds of the mobs that have broken into our homes and murdered our families and stolen all we have and blamed us for somehow fertilizing these crimes by our own actions.

No god has reigned down locusts or boils or vermin upon our oppressors to aid our escape.

It is our first born who bear the penalties prescribed.

It is our sons and daughters who sleep in the ground.

No god has ever intervened or stayed the sword of our executioners.

There will never be a 'when' for this so-called god's appearance, for this god is a figment, a confabulation, the fevered hallucination of desperation.

That being said, it is also fair and reasonable to ask, ***'What is a Jew without his god? Can such a thing exist?'***

Faith is such a temptress with her parables and her welcoming table.

Faith is a power beyond redemption or damnation that releases two golems into the world.

One golem lures us first into a somnolence which soon enough subsumes the belief itself and replaces it with the hollow gestures and integuments of ritual, and the other leads us to the mindless, voracious and insatiate appetite for hegemony and subjugation, conquest and the imperialism of conversion.

The Book of Genesis recounts the story of Abraham and Isaac who set out for Mount Moriah to perform an act of faith, a challenge placed before the old man by the one he called Yahweh. He was to take his son Isaac and slaughter him to show obedience to the will of this god. And as the story unfolded, Abraham raised the knife to do as he was bid, and an angel intervened and stayed his hand.

At this moment the paradigm of faith and belief and obedience collapsed and was shattered for all time, for Abraham failed the test entirely and in so doing showed Yahweh the ultimate ruin of his own creation; faith was revealed to be the cancer that has scourged the earth ever since.

If an "angel" can intercede between this god and his subjects, this god cannot be omnipotent and if this god is not omnipotent, it is not God.

And we reject the circular arguments that this god so instructed the angel to intervene, or any other postulate provided without evidence that seeks merely to keep the religious carousel of confusion in perpetual rotation.

But we do admire and revere the minds that created these parables in an effort to make the world a more peaceful and inhabitable place.

It is through the art of metaphor and analogy that we come face to face with the nature of our vexations.

It is to our discredit as a species that the interpretations of these stories have been annexed and twisted for the purposes of a vain and maleficent power claiming to speak for a divine creator.

The priest is not but a jackal who feeds on the spiritually destitute.

The biblical story of Abraham and Isaac was a clear warning to humankind of the dangers and pitfalls and ultimately the lethality of faith and obedience absent reason and good cause and yet it has been referred to time and time again as proof of Abraham's good character.

One who truly seeks freedom, seeks freedom from faith.

He seeks to abjure self-delusions and psychoses and even in some cases the very instincts borne deep of the past where they were needed for survival, before rational thinking began to bloom in the human brain and gave birth to the fruit of choice.

And what did the harlot Faith make of choice? Why, it cursed the apple of wisdom as the poison of deception, and then shackled womankind to the endless lie of perfidy, a lie that has followed her relentlessly through the ages, spurred on by those who would take advantage of her burden.

And yet for 3000 years we have held that a Jew is one who was "chosen" and "saved" by faith and miracles which are asserted to be evidence of Yahweh, (whose existence we are also told we must accept on faith, without evidence!)

The Jewish sage and prophet Robert Zimmerman, though at times profoundly insecure in his own beliefs questions the nature of practiced religious faith:

"With a time-rusted compass blade

Aladdin and his lamp
Sits with utopian hermit monks.
Side-saddle on the golden calf
And on their promises of paradise
You will not hear a laugh.
All except inside the gates of Eden."
(Bob Dylan, Gates of Eden)

So here we sit, contemplating an ancient myth, albeit one that has sustained us through some of the worst horrors men have visited upon each other, year after year, century after century, bloodbath after bloodbath.

ALL: ***"In every generation, they rise against us..."***

We can say without exaggeration we have faced the unrelenting hatred and calumnies of a seemingly endless list of enemies since the scattering of the ten tribes seven hundred years before the birth of the renegade Jew, Jesus, who would usher in a new species of misanthropy, namely: Deicide.

The lone tribe of Judah from which we all spring survived until the Babylonian exile and shortly thereafter the first attempt at total extermination under the Persians.

So, we ask, where is the god of the Passover?

Come forth. Raise thy strong hand. Where is thy outstretched arm?

In the time before the mythical Jesus, the mass murders begin under the Romans: 12,000 here; 50,000 there; until 600,000 are murdered by Hadrian ending the last of three wars between the Jews and the Romans in utter defeat for the Jews and their expulsion from the lands of Palestine into the arms of the world.

The diaspora begins.

ALL: ***'If not now, when?'***

Now comes the Christian Church accusing us of killing God, a crime that Jews will bear as the mark of Caine for the next 2000 years.

ALL: ***'If not now, when?'***

Exile, imprisonment, enslavement and slaughter after slaughter by Romans, Muslims, Christians. No punishment, no malice can be described that has not befallen us.

The Spanish church presents an entirely new meaning to the phrase, "act of faith," as it is used to describe their torture chambers and pyres where tens of thousands are burned alive.

ALL: ***'If not now, when?'***

Let the centuries pass, each one bloodier than the one before it.

Each time, the number of dead increases.

Each time the insidious oppressions multiply, until the Magnum Opus of mindless hatred explodes with the industrialized murder of six million who are gassed, burned, shot, buried alive, starved to death, injected with diseases, thrown from cliffs...one million of them children.

They walked into the flames, knelt before the killing pits, lined up dutifully at the train stations - handed over their children to be murdered - all the while singing praises to the great being that has brought them from Egyptian slavery but who has been absent ever since and now on the cusp of complete extinction, speaks with silence.

With the walls of the Warsaw Ghetto crumbling around them, amid the rain of bombs and blood and broken bodies, they bless the sabbath bread and the wine and candle; they recite the story of Passover; they open the door and beckon to Elijah the Prophet...

ALL: ***'If not now, when?'***

Enslaved by ritual and delusion, they cannot entertain the idea that their faith is a blind prison, their god-being does not exist and their sacrifices have been pointless.

The heavens are empty.

We have only ourselves.

Our return to the Land of Israel should have been the closing of the circle and for some years of relatively safe harbor we drifted in a daydream that the cycle had come to an end.

October 7, 2023.

ALL: ***'If not now, when?'***

When will we come to realize our salvation, if such is even possible, cannot and will not come from the world of belief and faith and false gods and hope and prayers and dreams and will never be permitted by those around us?

We have been chosen, not to be the light of the world but to be the bottomless receptacle of the world's malevolence by a malevolent world.

What more must we experience for Never Again to have true meaning?

So we must ask again, ***"what is a Jew without his god?"***

"...I am a Jew...If you poison us, do we not die?

And if you wrong us, shall we not revenge?
If we are like you in the rest,
we will resemble you in that.
The villainy you teach me,
I will execute,
and it shall go hard
but I will better the instruction..."
(Shakespeare, Merchant of Venice)

There have always been among us, those who break under the strain of this burden, who appropriate another costume of 'faith,' who swear allegiance to a foreign power whether by manning the ghettos and concentration camps as police and kapos and informers or by aligning themselves with enemies in the vain and pathetic hope that the hatred and derision can be dissolved by confessions and supplication. They display a hysterical contempt and hatred for their own people which they present as 'genuine love.' They impart credence to our enemies and revel in the attention they receive in return.

They seek to disavow and repudiate their birthright, but they disavow and repudiate only themselves; the arms of their erstwhile new allies are ripe with thorns; they will never be admitted into the home of 'the other,' and eventually they will be ripped from hiding, and left to wander the earth in a purgatory as traitors and liars, despised and mistrusted by all.

The list of these miscreants is a long one; may their names be forgotten.

October 7, 2023.

ALL: ***'If not now, when?'***

Not since the German propagated holocaust of World War 2 has there been a pogrom of the magnitude of October 7, 2023.

And yet, hundreds of thousands, if not millions have taken to the streets calling for Jewish blood once again because this attack on Israel is somehow justified.

The lies of our enemies are received as gifts and become the mantra of howling mobs while our protestations are drowned in contempt and derision.

Individuals whose malign intentions lay dormant through a thousand world tragedies, through the annihilation of millions of innocent victims of every stripe, who shrugged off and turned away from ten-thousand pleadings, from a hundred-thousand causes suddenly awaken to the one crusade that calls to them: *The Jew.*

We are told that more than half the American population between 18 and 26 is calling for the destruction of Israel and (therefore) the annihilation of the Jews.

American university campuses are overrun with venal mobs spewing Jew-hate indistinguishable from the epic accomplishments of the German Nazis and the administrators of these 'institutions of higher learning' declare it to be free speech.

Professors are "exhilarated' by the chants of death and the spilled blood.

An old man is beaten to death in the streets of Los Angeles.

Jewish women are raped, tortured to death, and mutilated in the tunnels of Hamas 'freedom fighters' and feminists the world over are completely silent despite multiple witness accounts. It takes months for the UN to acknowledge these events, while completely fabricated stories of IDF raping Palestinian women are published immediately without verification and eventually have to be withdrawn when the lie is exposed.

Jewish children are burned alive, and the world looks on!

The Red Cross tells the parents of children kidnapped and murdered by Hamas to ***'think about the Palestinians.'***

The perpetrators hide in the arms of their women and children, and we are told to let them be!

How can this be so?!

And yet, we know the answer.

It is always the same answer.

The old ones tell the story of the five gamblers playing a game in which individuals must assess the strength of their opponents without knowing what cards they hold. Each man bets according to his intuition, his assessment of the others. No factual information is exchanged. This one tweaks his nose; that one blinks rapidly; another frowns and clears his throat. Are these so-called 'tells' deliberate bluff? Are they irrelevant? Do they indicate strength? Weakness? Finally, though, the betting comes to an end, and one must show his cards to win. Some fold, without revealing anything about their hand. Some accept the challenge. Someone wins. As it turns out, one individual wins more often than the others. What can be made of this? Suspicion grows that this winning individual is cheating. Somehow, he knows when the others hold weak hands and when he should abjure. But no one can provide any evidence to support the charge of cheating because there is no evidence. The others cannot accept this. If they do, they must accept the fact that this man is better at the game, his intuition is more accurate and more reliable, his bluff is impenetrable. But they will not accept this and so they turn to the next explanation which is that the winner is abnormal, supernatural, in league with mysterious evil forces. No evidence is necessary to support this accusation because the wraith leave behind no sign by which mortal man might track them. The man is thrown from the game in a storm of ridicule and approbation. His reputation is marked. A yellow stripe is struck on his coat and must be clearly displayed so all may know that he is a servant of the devil, that they may scorn him.

No fact or truth or evidence has the slightest effect on the spirit of the mob.

They have complete faith in their beliefs.

And yet, we, sitting here tonight, have somehow survived, if for no other purpose than to remember these details and preserve them and hand them down to our descendants that they may be aware, that they may be vigilant, just as the deluded faithful have tried to do by recounting the Exodus fable, with all its ornamental ritual for almost 3000 years.

The angel of death has once again passed over our house and here we repose, isolate and abandoned in our terror, in melancholy, in pained relief.

Next time - ***and there will be a next time*** - we may be the ones dragged from our homes and immolated before the shrieking mob.

It may be our neighbors who will appear snarling at our door; erstwhile friends will come brandishing pitch and hangman's noose and some even wearing the Star of David will break down the doors preaching true love as they slaughter our children and divide our possessions among themselves.

But not tonight.

Tonight, others twist and turn in the boil-pot of Jew-hate, many crying out to their god for rescue.

He will not come, for he is not.

We have only ourselves.

The heavens are empty except for what we ourselves release into the ether.

(All raise a glass of wine)

ALL: ***We raise this glass of wine to the spirits of life on earth and say, 'we drink in gratitude and humility.'***

A bowl of water is passed around the table and each participant dips a finger into the bowl.

We wash our hands and come to this table with an open but a heavy heart, for this is a time of reflection, not celebration.

Our survival is not victory and we shall not dance on the graves of vanquished enemies.

A piece of parsley is distributed to each person.

The parsley is dipped into salt water and the participants say:

ALL: We remember our forefathers who tilled the soil and gave thanks for the earth's produce. The salt water reminds us that many tears have been shed over the millennia in slavery in its many forms and tears are shed this very night among those still so enthralled.

READER: Two stones repose on this seder plate. One stone reminds us of the dead, perished in uncountable ways and means and we bring this to their many graves. One stone reminds us that we are here, but we will die and all that will be left is how we lived and a stone to mark the grave.

This orange reminds us that the curse of Eve is the first calumny in religion's lexicon of repression and enslavement that has ever since plagued the earth and yet remains unrepentant in the wings of every society.

This tablespoon of sand reminds us of the Negev and the Sinai that we are of the desert and to the desert we shall return.

This piece of red cloth reminds us of the poppy that springs forth from the barren rocks that once owned the land and are raised in the rebirth of spring and ha Eretz.

(The middle matzah is removed from the three matzos of the seder plate and is broken into two pieces, one half being set aside.)

(The three matzos are held high.)

ALL: This is the bread of affliction, the simple bread our ancestors ate in the land of Egypt. If you are hungry, join us and we will know each other. Come in need but come in friendship. May bounty and peace come to Israel and all who love her.

Questions

Traditionally the youngest among us poses a question four times, with a different answer offered each time.

Why is this night different from all other nights?

The four answers add nothing to anyone's understanding except as shallow explanations of ritual behavior which has of course reached the aforementioned condition of supplanting entirely whatever it was meant to honor or memorialize in the first place.

If this night is to be different from all other nights, should it not pause us that we may reflect on matters of consequence impinging on our immediate lives and the lives of those in our midst?

It is the natural evolution of institutions that they soon enough seek to preserve themselves in disregard of the very people they were created to serve.

We have seen this in all aspects of life, whatever the form of government, whatever the national identity.

Religious institutions are no different.

The lord delivered us from Egypt, we are told and without his ***'mighty hand and outstretched arm',*** surely, we would still be slaves.

This lord's subsequent delinquency, his abrogation of the contract he supposedly set for himself is answered by the 'faithful' in the typically circular, inarticulate argument.

It was not the god who reneged, it was us. We have not been sufficiently adoring, we have not worshipped with enough zeal.

Our faith is false!

Endless circles of absurd commentary.

More significant is the discussion of the four sons: the wise, the wicked, the simple and the young.

The wicked son asks, ***'what do all these rituals mean to you?'*** consigning himself to social oblivion as one 'who would not be saved.'

And yet, is it not the wicked son who demands explanations for commitments and assignations that have delivered nothing but death and destruction for thousands of years?

We question these rituals not because we set ourselves apart from our tribe but because we demand that those in whom we shall place faith and trust, deliver on their promises.

It is not the wise son who remembers his duty to his people; he remembers only his duty to the rituals that have come to define them and blind obeisance to an apocryphal 'father' without concern for his offspring.

If a full cup of wine represents joy, we shall diminish it by pouring one drop out for every plague that has sought to destroy this same joy and continues tormenting humankind with unrelenting viciousness.

ONE: BLIND OBEDIENCE!

TWO: WILLFUL IGNORANCE!
THREE: INTOLLERANCE!
FOUR: HYPOCRISY!
FIVE: VENALITY!
SIX: CUPIDITY!
SEVEN: GREED!
EIGHT: MALICE!
NINE: SPITE!
TEN: MENDACITY!

READER: A rabbi approached a man and asked him, 'what is slavery?'

The man thought for a moment and answered, 'a slave is one who is forced to act against his will without compensation other than the lash.' The rabbi nodded and went on his way, but he was not completely satisfied with the answer. There seemed to be something missing. So, he asked a woman the same question and she said, unhesitatingly, 'a slave is one whose identity is taken from her and replaced with the desires of another.' Still unsatisfied, the rabbi asked a wealthy man the question. The man thought for a moment and replied, 'a slave is one who does not rebel, he is a coward, he fears death much more than life.' Still unhappy the rabbi went on his way. After a while he came upon a man working a field in a burning sun. He was clearly exhausted. The rabbi asked him, 'are you a slave?' The man thought for a moment and said, 'do not bother me with such questions, what good comes of knowing?" and went back to work.' The rabbi was struck by this answer, and he thought for a long while and then he realized that the answer to his question was not simple. A slave is one who may not choose his own path, he thought. He is called by another name that suits his master. He cowers in fear of retribution. The rabbi paled and began to shake. He had just described himself. Better not to know the answer, he decided and hurried into the night.

Better not to know the answer.

Around us this day there are those in bondage in myriad evil forms, young and old, man and woman of virtually every race and hue and age – every one held against his will, named and ordered by the master, bowed under the lash.

As we sit here tonight contemplating our good fortune, we shall ask this god to dismount his throne and come to our table and explain why any one being or force or entity with the power to ameliorate such monstrous behavior declines to do so.

We would ask him to repeat his great miracles of ancient times and loosen the bonds of all so kept.

But he will not come; for he is not.

The greatest test we will face comes when our self-defense convinces us that our enemies are not individuals making their own decisions but a volvox driven by an evil synchronicity.

We must guard against becoming what we most hate and fear.

No people can at once be both a part of the society in which they find themselves and apart from it.

Yea, we must reach out; we must open our doors to the stranger; we must offer refuge to those who *fall before our feet* until they show themselves to be unworthy.

Tikkun Olam – to heal the world.

In this too we are chosen, for the knowledge of right and wrong pierces all denial of same, and we cannot claim mana for ourselves and deny it to another.

"If I am not for myself, who will be for me? If I am only for myself, what am I?"

ALL: Next year in Jerusalem. Till then "we keep faith with those who sleep in the dust."

After the meal

Tradition holds that certain songs be sung and among them is the most famous and important Chad Gadya, (which is not really a song with a melody as much as it is a kind of Aramaic hip-hop) the lyrics for which are as follows:

One little goat
One little goat, one little goat
Which my father bought for two zuzim*
One little goat, one little goat
The cat came, and ate the goat
Which my father bought for two zuzim\
One little goat, one little goat
The dog came, and bit the cat, that ate the goat,
Which my father bought for two zuzim
One little goat, one little goat
The mother with stick came, and beat the dog
that bit the cat, that ate the goat,
Which my father bought for two zuzim
One little goat, one little goat
The fire came, and burned the stick
that beat the dog, that bit the cat, that ate the goat,
Which my father bought for two zuzim.
One little goat, one little goat

The water came, and extinguished the fire,
that burned the stick, that beat the dog
that bit the cat, that ate the goat
Which my father bought for two zuzim
One little goat, one little goat
The ox came, and drank the water,
that extinguished the fire, that burned the stick,
that beat the dog, that bit the cat, that ate the goat,
Which my father bought for two zuzim.
One little goat, one little goat
The slaughterer (Shohet) came, and killed the ox,
that drank the water, that extinguished the fire
that burned the stick, that beat the dog,
that bit the cat, that ate the goat,
Which my father bought for two zuzim
One little goat, one little goat
The angel of death came, and slew the slaughterer,
who killed the ox, that drank the water
that extinguished the fire, that burned the stick
that beat the dog, that bit the cat, that ate the goat,
Which my father bought for two zuzim
One little goat, one little goat
Then came the Holy One, Blessed be He
and smote the angel of death, who slew the slaughterer
who killed the ox, that drank the water
that extinguished the fire, that burned the stick
that beat the dog, that bit the cat, that ate the goat,
Which my father bought for two zuzim

One little goat, one little goat

Here are some others, including *Hey Dahankoye*, probably the most famous Zionist song from the 1930s in Russia and *Hatikva,* Israel's national anthem.

Hey Dahankoye, refers to a time in Russia, around 1932-1933 during which the communist government of Joseph Stalin forced farm collectivization on the Ukraine. For the Jews, this was the first time in hundreds of years that they were "allowed" to be farmers, a restricted occupation. Jews could not own land. They enthusiastically welcomed the change – hence the song's lyric:

Who said the Jews cannot be farmers,
Spit in his eye who would so harm us.

The collectivization, however, resulted in a man-made famine that killed around four million Ukrainian peasants. Starving men, woman and children were prevented by Stalin's army from leaving the Ukraine to look for food. Reports of cannibalism were not unusual. It is called the Holodomor and was seared into Ukrainian consciousness as the Holocaust was for Jews.

One of Stalin's chief enforcers of this catastrophe, Lazar Kaganowicz, considered one of Stalin's most enthusiastic henchmen, and at one point third in line of succession: (Stalin, Molotov, Kaganowicz) was a Jew the Ukrainians blame outright for the Holodomor.

The Ukrainians welcomed the Nazi invasion of 1941 and helped murder millions of Jews, with the memory of the famine fresh in their minds and the name Kaganowicz on their lips. The millions of innocent Jewish peasants, tailors and ragmen, rabbis, traders, musicians, poets they helped exterminate had nothing whatsoever to do with the Russian government, but to the Ukrainian, every Jew of every age, sex or disposition was Kaganowicz in the flesh, a communist apparatchik, and directly responsible for the catastrophe. Communism, collectivism and collaboration thus became welded to the word Jew.

Not that they needed an excuse.

The Ukrainians had been butchering Jews for decades in periodic pogroms.

The current situation (as of this writing, 2024) in Ukraine has flipped the narrative somewhat as the leader of Ukraine in its death-struggle with Russian invaders is the Jew, Volodymyr Zelensky.

The outcome of this war will likely determine how deep this new association between Ukrainians and Jews has taken hold. **

If Ukraine is forced to surrender or compromise significantly, the blame will fall directly on Zelensky and 'world Jewry.'

Success of course, will be seen to have been achieved *in spite* of him – and us.

****All the above is public record taken from open sources.*
Anyone wanting more information or
proof of accuracy need only type
a few words into the Google search engine.

Dzhankoye

Leadsheet

Arr. Lennard Farwick

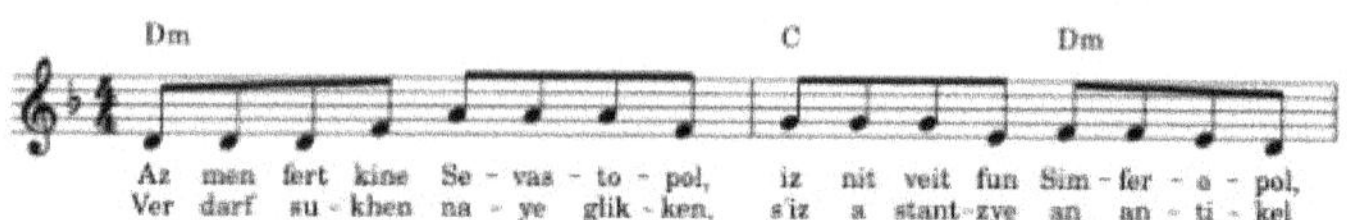

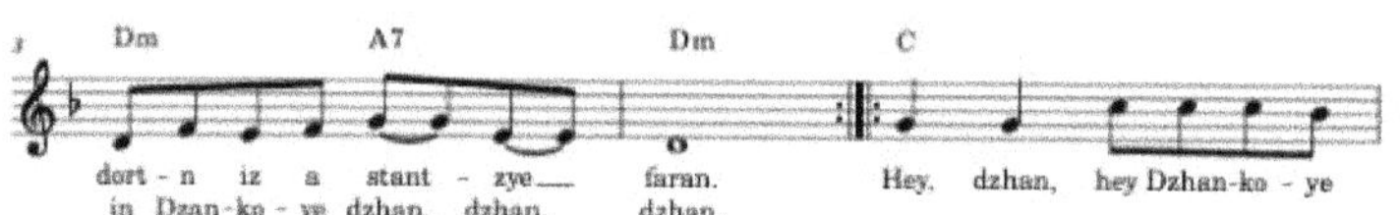

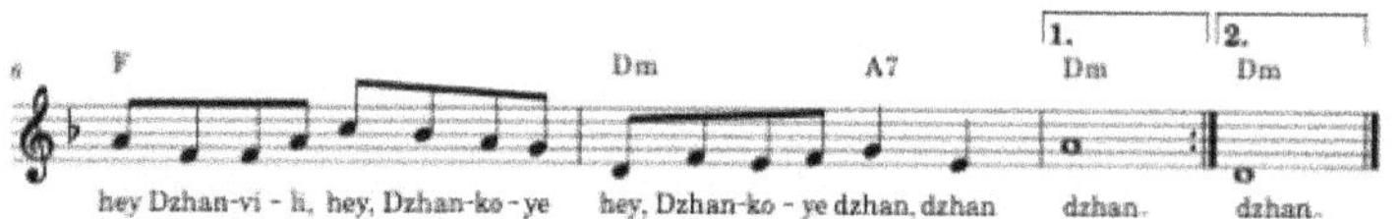

Enfert Yid'n af mine Kashe,
vi'z mayn bruder, vi'z Abrashe,
s'geyt bay ihm der traktor vi a bahn.
Di mume leye ba der kosilke
beyle ba der molotilke
In Dzhankoye, dzhan, dzhan, dzhan.
Hey, dzhan...

Ver zogt as yidn konen nor handlen
ess'n fette yoikh mit mandlen,
nor nit zenen kaynen arbetsman?
Dos konen zogn nor di sonim
Yid'n, shpayt zey on im ponim.
Tut a kuk af dzhan, dzhan, dzhan...
Hey, dzhan...

When you go from Sevastopol
on your way to Simferopol,
just you go a little farther down.
There's a little railroad depot
known quite well by all the people,
called Dzhankoye, dzhan, dzhan dzhan.
Hey, dzhan...

Now if you look for paradise
you'll see it there before your eyes.
Stop your search and go no farther on.
There we have a collective farm
all run by Jewish husky arms
at Dzhankoye, dzhan, dzhan, dzhan.
Hey, dzhan...

Aunt Natasha drives the tractor
Grandma runs the cream extractor
while we work we all can sing our songs.
Who says that Jews cannot be farmers?
Spit in his eye, who would so harm us.
Tell him of Dzhankoye, dzhan, dzhan.
Hey dzhan...

The Hope

As long as deep within the heart
A Jewish soul stirs,
And forward, to the ends of the East
An eye looks out, towards Zion.
Our hope is not yet lost,
The hope of two thousand years,
To be a free people in our land
The land of Zion and Jerusalem
https://lyricstranslate.com

Hatikva
Poem by: Naftali Herz Imber
♩ = 70
Piano
Pno.

This is a piece from Morocco, in itself a complicated history. Of 250,000 Jews at its height, there remain about 2,000.

In our village Todra

na na na na na na na
ti na na na na na
In our village Todra, in the heart of the Atlas Mountains
We would take the child when it reaches 5 years of age
A crown of flowers we'd give to him, at our village Todra
With a crown on his head we adorn him, when he turns
5
all the children in the street bid him to a great feast
when he turns 5, in our little village Todra

na noi noi noi noi noi..

(SOLO)
and so the birthday boy when he reaches age 5
at our little village Todra we bring him to Synagogue
and we write on a wooden board from Alef to Tav
all the letters in honey, and tell him: lick it, my friend..
and the Torahin his mouth feels sweet as honey
in our little village Todra, in the heart of the Atlas Range

AFTERWORD

This year's Synod of the illuminati and the Elders of Zion will be held in Upstate New York, the actual location kept secret until the appointed day for security reasons.

The Mossad oversees the safety of the community, as usual.

The caterer has assured us of a large smorgasbord of Christian children for the Matzo session and others can be cooked to order.

If you have dietary restrictions, please contact Satan directly.

Phone: 666-666-6666

New email:

NoMercy@Hellsapoppin.org

RSVP.

Shalom.

Timeline of antisemitism in the 20th century

From Wikipedia, the free encyclopedia

*This is a **dynamic list**[1] and may never be able to satisfy particular standards for completeness. You can help by **adding missing items**[2] with **reliable sources**[3].*

This **timeline of antisemitism** chronicles the facts of **antisemitism**[4], hostile actions or discrimination against Jews as a religious or ethnic group, in the 20th century. It includes events in the history of antisemitic thought, actions taken to combat or relieve the effects of antisemitism, and events that affected the prevalence of antisemitism in later years. The **history of antisemitism**[5] can be traced from ancient times to the present day.

For events specifically pertaining to the expulsion of Jews, see **Jewish refugees**[6].

In the late 19th and early 20th centuries, the **Roman Catholic Church**[7] adhered to a distinction between "good antisemitism" and "bad antisemitism". The "bad" kind promoted hatred of Jews because of their descent. This was considered un-Christian because the Christian message was intended for all of humanity regardless of ethnicity; anyone could become a Christian. The "good" kind criticized alleged Jewish conspiracies to control newspapers, banks, and other

---

1. *https://en.wikipedia.org/wiki/Wikipedia:WikiProject_Lists#Dynamic_lists*
2. *https://en.wikipedia.org/wiki/Special:EditPage/Timeline_of_antisemitism_in_the_20th_century*
3. *https://en.wikipedia.org/wiki/Wikipedia:Reliable_sources*
4. https://en.wikipedia.org/wiki/Antisemitism
5. https://en.wikipedia.org/wiki/History_of_antisemitism
6. https://en.wikipedia.org/wiki/Jewish_refugees
7. https://en.wikipedia.org/wiki/Roman_Catholic_Church

institutions, to care only about accumulation of wealth, etc. Many Catholic bishops wrote articles criticizing Jews on such grounds, and, when accused of promoting hatred of Jews, would remind people that they condemned the "bad" kind of antisemitism.[1][8]

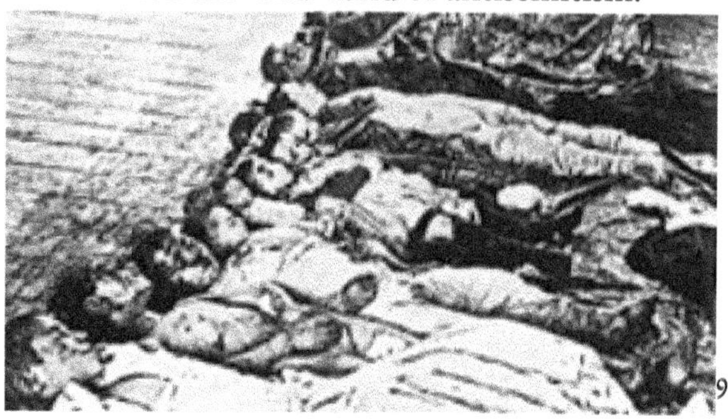
[9]

The victims of a 1905 pogrom in **Yekaterinoslav**[10]

1900s[edit[11]]

1903

The **Kishinev pogrom**[12]. 49 Jews murdered.

1903

The first publication of ***The Protocols of the Elders of Zion***[13] **hoax**[14] in St. Petersburg, Russia (by **Pavel Krushevan**[15]).

8. https://en.wikipedia.org/wiki/Timeline_of_antisemitism_in_the_20th_century#cite_note-1
9. https://en.wikipedia.org/wiki/File:Ekaterinoslav1905.jpg
10. https://en.wikipedia.org/wiki/Dnipro
11. https://en.wikipedia.org/w/index.php?title=Timeline_of_antisemitism_in_the_20th_century&action=edit§ion=1
12. https://en.wikipedia.org/wiki/Kishinev_pogrom
13. *https://en.wikipedia.org/wiki/The_Protocols_of_the_Elders_of_Zion*
14. https://en.wikipedia.org/wiki/Hoax
15. https://en.wikipedia.org/wiki/Pavel_Krushevan

1904

The **Limerick boycott**[16] was an economic boycott waged against the small Jewish community in Limerick, Ireland. It was accompanied by a number of assaults, stone throwing and intimidation, which caused many Jews to leave the city.

1905

Pogrom in **Yekaterinoslav**[17]. 66 Jews were killed and 125 wounded and Jewish homes and shops were looted.[2][18]

1905

The **1905 Kiev pogrom**[19] was a massacre of 100 Jews.

1906

Alfred Dreyfus[20] was exonerated and reinstated as a major in the French Army.

1907

---

16. https://en.wikipedia.org/wiki/Limerick_boycott

17. https://en.wikipedia.org/wiki/Dnipro

18. https://en.wikipedia.org/wiki/Timeline_of_antisemitism_in_the_20th_century#cite_note-2

19. https://en.wikipedia.org/wiki/1905_Kiev_pogrom

20. https://en.wikipedia.org/wiki/Alfred_Dreyfus

Over 60 Jews in the **Mellah**[21] of **Casablanca**[22] are killed in a pogrom by **Kabyle**[23] **Muslims**[24]. Many more were wounded, and a large number of women and children were carried off.[3][25]

1909

Salomon Reinach[26] and Florence Simmonds refer to "this *new antisemitism*, masquerading as patriotism, which was first propagated at **Berlin**[27] by the court chaplain **Stöcker**[28], with the connivance of Bismarck."[4][29] Similarly, **Peter N. Stearns**[30] comments that "the ideology behind the new anti-Semitism [in Germany] was more racist than religious."[5][31]

1910

21. https://en.wikipedia.org/wiki/Mellah
22. https://en.wikipedia.org/wiki/Casablanca
23. https://en.wikipedia.org/wiki/Kabyle_people
24. https://en.wikipedia.org/wiki/Muslims
25. https://en.wikipedia.org/wiki/Timeline_of_antisemitism_in_the_20th_century#cite_note-3
26. https://en.wikipedia.org/wiki/Salomon_Reinach
27. https://en.wikipedia.org/wiki/Berlin
28. https://en.wikipedia.org/wiki/Adolf_Stoecker
29. https://en.wikipedia.org/wiki/Timeline_of_antisemitism_in_the_20th_century#cite_note-4
30. https://en.wikipedia.org/wiki/Peter_N._Stearns
31. https://en.wikipedia.org/wiki/Timeline_of_antisemitism_in_the_20th_century#cite_note-5

The **1910 Shiraz blood libel**[32] was a pogrom of the Jewish quarter in **Shiraz**[33], Iran. It was sparked by accusations that the Jews had **ritually murdered a Muslim girl**[34]. By the end of the pogrom, 12 Jews were killed, 50 or so were wounded, and 6,000 were robbed of all their possessions.

1912

The Tritl[35] or the **1912 Fez massacre**[36] left 42 **Moroccan Jews**[37] dead.

1913

The **Blood libel**[38] trial of **Menahem Mendel Beilis**[39] in Kiev.

1915

In one 48-hour interval in May 1915, all 40,000 Jews living in **Kaunas**[40], **Lithuania**[41] are forcibly removed from the city.[6][42]

---

32. https://en.wikipedia.org/wiki/1910_Shiraz_blood_libel
33. https://en.wikipedia.org/wiki/Shiraz
34. https://en.wikipedia.org/wiki/Blood_Libel
35. https://en.wikipedia.org/wiki/The_Tritl
36. https://en.wikipedia.org/wiki/1912_Fez_massacre
37. https://en.wikipedia.org/wiki/Moroccan_Jews
38. https://en.wikipedia.org/wiki/Blood_libel
39. https://en.wikipedia.org/wiki/Menahem_Mendel_Beilis
40. https://en.wikipedia.org/wiki/Kaunas
41. https://en.wikipedia.org/wiki/Lithuania
42. https://en.wikipedia.org/wiki/Timeline_of_antisemitism_in_the_20th_century#cite_note-6

1915

The **Leo Frank**[43] trial and **lynching**[44] in **Atlanta**[45], Georgia turns the spotlight on **antisemitism in the United States**[46] and leads to the founding of the **Anti-Defamation League**[47].

1917

The **1917 Jaffa deportation**[48] was a forceful expulsion and confiscation of property of 10,000 Jews from Jaffa and Tel Aviv by Ottoman authorities.

1917–1921

Attacked for being revolutionaries or counter-revolutionaries, unpatriotic pacifists or warmongers, religious zealots or godless atheists, capitalist exploiters or bourgeois profiteers, masses of Jewish civilians were **murdered in pogroms**[49] in the course of **Russian Civil War**[50] (by various estimates 70,000 to 250,000, the number of orphans exceeded 300,000).

1918

3,000–10,000 **Mountain Jews**[51] are killed during **March Days**[52].

1918

The **Lwów pogrom of 1918**[53] was an attack on the Jewish population of **Lwów**[54] that took place on 21–23 November 1918

---

43. https://en.wikipedia.org/wiki/Leo_Frank
44. https://en.wikipedia.org/wiki/Lynching
45. https://en.wikipedia.org/wiki/Atlanta
46. https://en.wikipedia.org/wiki/Antisemitism_in_the_United_States
47. https://en.wikipedia.org/wiki/Anti-Defamation_League
48. https://en.wikipedia.org/wiki/1917_Jaffa_deportation
49. https://en.wikipedia.org/wiki/Pogroms_of_the_Russian_Civil_War
50. https://en.wikipedia.org/wiki/Russian_Civil_War
51. https://en.wikipedia.org/wiki/Mountain_Jews
52. https://en.wikipedia.org/wiki/March_Days

during the **Polish–Ukrainian War**[55]. After the pogrom was over, an estimated 52–150 Jewish residents were killed and hundreds were injured.

1919

The **Kiev pogroms of 1919**[56] were a series of pogroms in various places around **Kiev**[57] carried out by **White Volunteer Army**[58] troops. There were a total of 1,326 pogroms across Ukraine around that time, in which between 30,000 and 70,000 Jews were massacred. According to some estimates, the pogroms left half a million Jews homeless. The series of events occurred in the following districts:

1919

The **Pinsk massacre**[59] was the mass execution of thirty-five Jewish residents of **Pinsk**[60] on 5 April 1919 by the Polish Army.

1919

In February 1919 a brigade of **UNR**[61] troops killed 1500 Jews in **Proskurov**[62].[7][63]

1919

53. https://en.wikipedia.org/wiki/Lw%C3%B3w_pogrom_of_1918
54. https://en.wikipedia.org/wiki/Lw%C3%B3w
55. https://en.wikipedia.org/wiki/Polish%E2%80%93Ukrainian_War
56. https://en.wikipedia.org/wiki/Kiev_pogroms_of_1919
57. https://en.wikipedia.org/wiki/Kiev
58. https://en.wikipedia.org/w/index.php?title=White_Volunteer_Army&action=edit&redlink=1
59. https://en.wikipedia.org/wiki/Pinsk_massacre
60. https://en.wikipedia.org/wiki/Pinsk
61. https://en.wikipedia.org/wiki/Ukrainian_People%27s_Republic
62. https://en.wikipedia.org/wiki/Proskurov_pogrom
63. https://en.wikipedia.org/wiki/Timeline_of_antisemitism_in_the_20th_century#cite_note-Vital-7

In **Tetiev**[64] on 25 March 1919, Cossack troops under the command of Colonels Cherkovsky, Kurovsky and Shliatoshenko murdered 4,000 Jews.[8][65]

1919–1920

During the **Russian Civil War**[66] the Jews of **Uman**[67] in eastern **Podolia**[68] were subjected to two **pogroms**[69] in 1919, as the town changed hands several times. The first pogrom, in spring, claimed 170 victims; the second one, in summer, more than 90. This time the Christian inhabitants helped to hide the Jews. The Council for Public Peace, with a Christian majority and a Jewish minority, saved the city from danger several times. In 1920, for example, it stopped the pogrom initiated by the troops of General **Denikin**[70].[9][71]

1919–1922

Soviet **Yevsektsiya**[72] (the Jewish section of the Communist Party) attacks **Bund**[73] and Zionist parties for "Jewish cultural particularism".

---

64. https://en.wikipedia.org/w/index.php?title=Tetiev_pogrom&action=edit&redlink=1

65. https://en.wikipedia.org/wiki/Timeline_of_antisemitism_in_the_20th_century#cite_note-Midlarsky-8

66. https://en.wikipedia.org/wiki/Russian_Civil_War

67. https://en.wikipedia.org/wiki/Uman

68. https://en.wikipedia.org/wiki/Podolia

69. https://en.wikipedia.org/wiki/Pogrom

70. https://en.wikipedia.org/wiki/Anton_Denikin

71. https://en.wikipedia.org/wiki/Timeline_of_antisemitism_in_the_20th_century#cite_note-9

72. https://en.wikipedia.org/wiki/Yevsektsiya

In April 1920, the All-Russian Zionist Congress is broken up by **Cheka**[74] led by **Bolsheviks**[75], whose leadership and ranks included many anti-Jewish Jews. Thousands are arrested and sent to **Gulag**[76] for "counter-revolutionary... collusion in the interests of Anglo-French bourgeoisie... to restore the Palestine state." **Hebrew language**[77] is banned, Judaism is suppressed, along with other religions.

The **Jerusalem pogrom of April 1920**[78] of old **Yishuv**[79].

The idea that the **Bolshevik revolution**[80] was a Jewish **conspiracy**[81] for the **world domination**[82] sparks worldwide interest in a fabricated text, ***The Protocols of the Elders of Zion***[83]. In a single year, five editions are sold out in England alone. In the US **Henry Ford**[84] prints 500,000 copies.

In the spring of 1920, **Henry Ford**[85] made his personal newspaper, ***The Dearborn Independent***[86], chronicle what he considered the "Jewish menace". Every week for 91 issues, the paper exposed some sort of Jewish-inspired evil major story in a headline. The most popular and

73. https://en.wikipedia.org/wiki/General_Jewish_Labor_Union
74. https://en.wikipedia.org/wiki/Cheka
75. https://en.wikipedia.org/wiki/Bolshevik
76. https://en.wikipedia.org/wiki/Gulag
77. https://en.wikipedia.org/wiki/Hebrew_language
78. https://en.wikipedia.org/wiki/1920_Nebi_Musa_riots
79. https://en.wikipedia.org/wiki/Yishuv
80. https://en.wikipedia.org/wiki/Bolshevik_revolution
81. https://en.wikipedia.org/wiki/Conspiracy_theory
82. https://en.wikipedia.org/wiki/Hegemony
83. *https://en.wikipedia.org/wiki/The_Protocols_of_the_Elders_of_Zion*
84. https://en.wikipedia.org/wiki/Henry_Ford
85. https://en.wikipedia.org/wiki/Henry_Ford
86. *https://en.wikipedia.org/wiki/The_Dearborn_Independent*

aggressive stories were then chosen to be reprinted into four volumes called ***The International Jew***[87].[10][88]

All **Jews in Mongolia**[89] are expelled by Russian anti-Bolshevik forces retreating after being defeated in Central Asia.[11][90]1

Jaffa riots[91] in Palestine.

1 921–1925

Outbreak of antisemitism in United States, led by **Ku Klux Klan**[92].

22

Soviet **Yevsektsiya**[93] (the Jewish section of the Communist Party) attacks **Bund**[94] and Zionist parties for "Jewish cultural particularism". In April 1920, the All-Russian Zionist Congress is broken up by **Cheka**[95] led by **Bolsheviks**[96], whose leadership and ranks included many anti-Jewish Jews. Thousands are arrested and sent to **Gulag**[97] for "counter-revolutionary... collusion in the interests of Anglo-French bourgeoisie... to restore the Palestine state." **Hebrew language**[98] is banned, Judaism is suppressed, along with other religions.**1922**

---

87. *https://en.wikipedia.org/wiki/The_International_Jew*
88. https://en.wikipedia.org/wiki/Timeline_of_antisemitism_in_the_20th_century#cite_note-10
89. https://en.wikipedia.org/wiki/History_of_the_Jews_in_Central_Asia
90. https://en.wikipedia.org/wiki/Timeline_of_antisemitism_in_the_20th_century#cite_note-11
91. https://en.wikipedia.org/wiki/Jaffa_riots
92. https://en.wikipedia.org/wiki/Ku_Klux_Klan
93. https://en.wikipedia.org/wiki/Yevsektsiya
94. https://en.wikipedia.org/wiki/General_Jewish_Labor_Union
95. https://en.wikipedia.org/wiki/Cheka
96. https://en.wikipedia.org/wiki/Bolshevik
97. https://en.wikipedia.org/wiki/Gulag
98. https://en.wikipedia.org/wiki/Hebrew_language

The government of Yemen, under **Yahya Muhammad Hamid ed-Din**[99], re-introduced an Islamic law entitled the "orphans decree". The law dictated that if Jewish boys or girls under the age of 12 were orphaned, they were to be forcibly converted to **Islam**[100], their connections to their families and communities were to be severed, and they had to be handed over to Muslim foster families.

1923

Der Stürmer[101] (pronounced **[deːɐ̯ ˈʃtʏʁmɐ]**[102], lit. "the Attacker") was a weekly **tabloid-format**[103] **Nazi**[104] newspaper published by **Julius Streicher**[105] (a prominent official in the **Nazi Party**[106]) from 1923 to the end of **World War II**[107], with brief suspensions in publication due to legal difficulties. It was a significant part of **Nazi propaganda**[108] and was vehemently anti-Semitic. **924**

The **National Origins Quota of 1924**[109] and **Immigration Act of 1924**[110] largely halted immigration to the U.S. from Eastern Europe and Russia; this was meant to restrict Eastern European Jews among

---

99. https://en.wikipedia.org/wiki/Yahya_Muhammad_Hamid_ed-Din
100. https://en.wikipedia.org/wiki/Islam
101. https://en.wikipedia.org/wiki/Der_St%C3%BCrmer
102. https://en.wikipedia.org/wiki/Help:IPA/Standard_German
103. https://en.wikipedia.org/wiki/Tabloid_(newspaper_format)
104. https://en.wikipedia.org/wiki/Nazism
105. https://en.wikipedia.org/wiki/Julius_Streicher
106. https://en.wikipedia.org/wiki/Nazi_Party
107. https://en.wikipedia.org/wiki/World_War_II
108. https://en.wikipedia.org/wiki/Nazi_propaganda
109. https://en.wikipedia.org/wiki/National_Origins_Quota_of_1924
110. https://en.wikipedia.org/wiki/Immigration_Act_of_1924

others, as a great many of these immigrants coming from Russia and Eastern Europe were Jews (the "outbreak of antisemitism" mentioned in the above entry may have also played a part in the passage of these acts).**1925**

The Ku Klux Klan in Prophecy[111] is a 144-page book written by Bishop **Alma Bridwell White**[112] in 1925 and illustrated by Reverend **Branford Clarke**[113].**[13]**114**[14]**115 This book primarily espouses White's deep fear and hatred of the **Roman Catholic Church**[116] while also promoting antisemitism, racism against African Americans, **white supremacy**[117], and **women's equality**[118].**[15]**119**[16]**120**[17]**121

Adolf Hitler[122] publishes ***Mein Kampf***[123].**1927**

---

111. *https://en.wikipedia.org/wiki/The_Ku_Klux_Klan_in_Prophecy*
112. https://en.wikipedia.org/wiki/Alma_Bridwell_White
113. https://en.wikipedia.org/wiki/Branford_Clarke
114. https://en.wikipedia.org/wiki/Timeline_of_antisemitism_in_the_20th_century#cite_note-neal-13
115. https://en.wikipedia.org/wiki/Timeline_of_antisemitism_in_the_20th_century#cite_note-ferguson-14
116. https://en.wikipedia.org/wiki/Catholic_Church
117. https://en.wikipedia.org/wiki/White_supremacy
118. https://en.wikipedia.org/wiki/Women%27s_equality
119. https://en.wikipedia.org/wiki/Timeline_of_antisemitism_in_the_20th_century#cite_note-15
120. https://en.wikipedia.org/wiki/Timeline_of_antisemitism_in_the_20th_century#cite_note-16
121. https://en.wikipedia.org/wiki/Timeline_of_antisemitism_in_the_20th_century#cite_note-17
122. https://en.wikipedia.org/wiki/Adolf_Hitler

The ***Schwartzbard trial***[124] was a sensational 1927 French murder trial that resulted in a **mistrial**[125] of international proportions. At the trial **Sholom Schwartzbard**[126] was accused of murdering the **Ukrainian**[127] immigrant and head of the Ukrainian government-in-exile **Symon Petlura**[128] in Paris. While the defendant fully admitted to the crime the trial at the end turned in accusation of Petlura's responsibility for the massive 1919–1920 **pogroms in Ukraine**[129] in which Schwartzbard had lost all 15 members of his family. Instead of Schwartzbard's murder case the trial was turned into a political case against the Ukrainian government. Schwartzbard was acquitted**28**

The **Massena blood libel**[130] was an instance of **blood libel**[131] against Jews in which the Jews of **Massena**[132], New York, were falsely accused of the **kidnapping**[133] and **ritual murder**[134] of a **Christian**[135] girl in September 1928

---

123. *https://en.wikipedia.org/wiki/Mein_Kampf*
124. *https://en.wikipedia.org/wiki/Schwartzbard_trial*
125. https://en.wikipedia.org/wiki/Mistrial_(law)
126. https://en.wikipedia.org/wiki/Sholom_Schwartzbard
127. https://en.wikipedia.org/wiki/Ukrainians
128. https://en.wikipedia.org/wiki/Symon_Petlura
129. https://en.wikipedia.org/wiki/Pogroms_in_Ukraine
130. https://en.wikipedia.org/wiki/Massena_blood_libel
131. https://en.wikipedia.org/wiki/Blood_libel
132. https://en.wikipedia.org/wiki/Massena_(village),_New_York
133. https://en.wikipedia.org/wiki/Kidnapping
134. https://en.wikipedia.org/wiki/Ritual_murder
135. https://en.wikipedia.org/wiki/Christians

The ancient Jewish community of **Hebron**[136] is **massacred by local Muslims**[137] over rumors that the Jews were planning to seize control of the **Temple Mount**[138].[19][139]

18–20 Jewish residents of **Safed**[140] were brutally killed in the **1929 Palestine riots**[141]

Pogrom[142] against the Jews of **Bălți**[143].[20][144] **August**

Christie Pits riot[145] takes place in **Toronto**[146], Ontario.[21][147]

In a series of lectures delivered at the **University of Virginia**[148] in 1933, published under the title *After Strange Gods: A Primer of Modern Heresy* (1934), **T.S. Eliot**[149] wrote of societal tradition and coherence,

---

136. https://en.wikipedia.org/wiki/Hebron
137. https://en.wikipedia.org/wiki/1929_Hebron_massacre
138. https://en.wikipedia.org/wiki/Temple_Mount
139. https://en.wikipedia.org/wiki/Timeline_of_antisemitism_in_the_20th_century#cite_note-19
140. https://en.wikipedia.org/wiki/Safed
141. https://en.wikipedia.org/wiki/1929_Palestine_riots
142. https://en.wikipedia.org/wiki/Pogrom
143. https://en.wikipedia.org/wiki/B%C4%83l%C8%9Bi
144. https://en.wikipedia.org/wiki/Timeline_of_antisemitism_in_the_20th_century#cite_note-20
145. https://en.wikipedia.org/wiki/Christie_Pits_riot
146. https://en.wikipedia.org/wiki/Toronto
147. https://en.wikipedia.org/wiki/Timeline_of_antisemitism_in_the_20th_century#cite_note-21
148. https://en.wikipedia.org/wiki/University_of_Virginia
149. https://en.wikipedia.org/wiki/T.S._Eliot

"What is still more important [than cultural homogeneity] is unity of religious background, and reasons of race and religion combine to make any large number of free-thinking Jews undesirable."[22][150] Eliot never re-published this book/lecture.[23][151] **933–1941**

Persecution of Jews in Germany rises until they are stripped of their rights not only as citizens, but also as human beings. During this time antisemitism reached its all-time high.[24][152]

◈ Law against Overcrowding of German Schools and Universities

◈ Law for the Reestablishment of the Professional Civil Service (ban on professions)

◈ The **Reich Flight Tax**[153] is used to expropriate funds from Jewish émigrés.2,000 **Afghani**[154] Jews are expelled from their towns and forced to live in the wilderness. **934**

The **1934 Thrace pogroms**[155] were a series of violent attacks that occurred in **Tekirdağ**[156], **Edirne**[157], **Kırklareli**[158], and **Çanakkale**[159]. Over 15,000 Jews had to flee from the region.**34**

---

150. https://en.wikipedia.org/wiki/Timeline_of_antisemitism_in_the_20th_century#cite_note-22
151. https://en.wikipedia.org/wiki/Timeline_of_antisemitism_in_the_20th_century#cite_note-Dean-23
152. https://en.wikipedia.org/wiki/Timeline_of_antisemitism_in_the_20th_century#cite_note-24
153. https://en.wikipedia.org/wiki/Reich_Flight_Tax
154. https://en.wikipedia.org/wiki/Afghanistan
155. https://en.wikipedia.org/wiki/1934_Thrace_pogroms
156. https://en.wikipedia.org/wiki/Tekirda%C4%9F
157. https://en.wikipedia.org/wiki/Edirne
158. https://en.wikipedia.org/wiki/K%C4%B1rklareli
159. https://en.wikipedia.org/wiki/%C3%87anakkale

34 **Algerian Jews**[160] were killed and hundreds were injured by Muslim mobs during the **1934 Constantine pogrom**[161]. 200 Jewish stores were raided, the total property damage was estimated at over 150 million Poincare francs. It also sent a quarter of Constantine's Jewish population into poverty.[25][162]

The first appearance of **The Franklin Prophecy**[163] on the pages of **William Dudley Pelley**[164]'s pro-Nazi weekly magazine *Liberation*. According to the **US Congress**[165] report:

Nuremberg Laws[166] introduced. Jewish rights rescinded. The Reich Citizenship Law strips them of citizenship. The Law for the Protection of German Blood and German Honor:

◈ Marriages between Jews and citizens of German or kindred blood are forbidden.

◈ Sexual relations outside marriage between Jews and nationals of German or kindred blood are forbidden.

◈ Jews will not be permitted to employ female citizens of German or kindred blood as domestic servants. forbidden to display the Reich and national flag or the national colors. On the other hand, they are permitted to display the Jewish colors.**1936**

The Bloody Day in Jaffa[167] refers to various violent attacks on Jews in **Jaffa**[168] by mobs of Muslims. **936**

---

160. https://en.wikipedia.org/wiki/Algerian_Jews

161. https://en.wikipedia.org/wiki/1934_Constantine_pogrom

162. https://en.wikipedia.org/wiki/Timeline_of_antisemitism_in_the_20th_century#cite_note-RLevy-25

163. https://en.wikipedia.org/wiki/The_Franklin_Prophecy

164. https://en.wikipedia.org/wiki/William_Dudley_Pelley

165. https://en.wikipedia.org/wiki/US_Congress

166. https://en.wikipedia.org/wiki/Nuremberg_Laws

167. https://en.wikipedia.org/wiki/The_Bloody_Day_in_Jaffa

The **Przytyk pogrom**[169] was an altercation between Jewish and Polish peasants, ending with two Jews and one Pole dead. **936**

Cardinal **August Hlond**[170], as Primate of Poland issued a pastoral letter on Catholic moral principles.[29][171] The long (5600-word) letter covered Catholic ethics policy, ethics principles and a section on "sins" (*Z Naszych Grzechów*) that addressed Christian shortcomings to **love one's neighbours**[172] in accordance with God's law. The latter section included a brief discussion of the "Jewish problem" (*Problem żydowski*): "So long as Jews remain Jews, a Jewish problem exists and will continue to exist (...) It is a fact that Jews are waging war against the Catholic church, that they are steeped in free-thinking, and constitute the vanguard of atheism, the Bolshevik movement, and revolutionary activity. It is a fact that Jews have a corruptive influence on morals and that their publishing houses are spreading pornography. It is true that Jews are perpetrating fraud, practicing usury, and dealing in prostitution. It is true that, from a religious and ethical point of view, Jewish youth are having a negative influence on the Catholic youth in our schools."[30][173] Hlond tempered these remarks with an admission that "not all Jews are this way" and forbade assaults on Jews or attacks

168. https://en.wikipedia.org/wiki/Jaffa

169. https://en.wikipedia.org/wiki/Przytyk_pogrom

170. https://en.wikipedia.org/wiki/August_Hlond

171. https://en.wikipedia.org/wiki/Timeline_of_antisemitism_in_the_20th_century#cite_note-29

172. https://en.wikipedia.org/wiki/Second_greatest_commandment

173. https://en.wikipedia.org/wiki/Timeline_of_antisemitism_in_the_20th_century#cite_note-modras-30

on their property. Yet, despite a warning to Catholics not to take an anti-Jewish moral stance, interspersed in the letter's words of friendship was an explicit condemnation of Jewish culture and also Judaism for its rejection of **Jesus Christ**[174]: "It is good to prefer your own kind when shopping, to avoid Jewish stores and Jewish stalls in the marketplace (...) One should stay away from the harmful moral influence of Jews, keep away from their anti-Christian culture, and especially boycott the Jewish press and demoralizing Jewish publications. (...) We do not honor the indescribable tragedy of that nation, which was the guardian of the idea of the **Messiah**[175] and from which was born the Savior. When divine mercy enlightens a Jew to sincerely accept his and our Messiah, let us greet him into our Christian ranks with joy."**[30]**[176] Hlond's letter was criticized by Polish Jewish groups who saw it as offering support and a rationalization for antisemitism.**[31]**[177] What also caught the attention of historians was the remark about not hating anyone, "not even Jews", implying "not even enemies". Were Jews to be loved as neighbors or enemies?**[32]**[178] However, while Hlond promoted the expulsion of German civilians after World War II, he

---

174. **https://en.wikipedia.org/wiki/Christ**

175. **https://en.wikipedia.org/wiki/Christ**

176. **https://en.wikipedia.org/wiki/Timeline_of_antisemitism_in_the_20th_century#cite_note-modras-30**

177. **https://en.wikipedia.org/wiki/Timeline_of_antisemitism_in_the_20th_century#cite_note-31**

178. **https://en.wikipedia.org/wiki/Timeline_of_antisemitism_in_the_20th_century#cite_note-32**

had always consistently condemned the Nazi persecution of the Jews.[*citation needed*179]

1937

"**The Eternal Jew**[180]" was the title of an exhibition of **degenerate art**[181] (*entartete Kunst*) displayed at the Library of the **German Museum**[182] in Munich from 8 November 1937 to 31 January 1938. The exhibition attracted 412,300 visitors, over 5,000 per day.[33]183

Ecuador[184] issues an order that states all **Ecuadorian Jewish**[185] residents not working in agriculture need to leave the country.[34]186

Anschluss[187], **pogroms**[188] in Vienna, anti-Jewish legislation, deportations to **Nazi concentration camps**[189].

---

179. *https://en.wikipedia.org/wiki/Wikipedia:Citation_needed*

180. https://en.wikipedia.org/wiki/The_Eternal_Jew_(art_exhibition)

181. https://en.wikipedia.org/wiki/Degenerate_art

182. https://en.wikipedia.org/wiki/German_Museum

183. https://en.wikipedia.org/wiki/Timeline_of_antisemitism_in_the_20th_century#cite_note-HolocaustResearchProject-33

184. https://en.wikipedia.org/wiki/Ecuador

185. https://en.wikipedia.org/wiki/History_of_the_Jews_in_Ecuador

186. https://en.wikipedia.org/wiki/Timeline_of_antisemitism_in_the_20th_century#cite_note-34

187. https://en.wikipedia.org/wiki/Anschluss

188. https://en.wikipedia.org/wiki/Pogroms

189. https://en.wikipedia.org/wiki/Nazi_concentration_camps

◈ Decree authorizing local authorities to bar Jews from the streets on certain days

◈ Decree empowering the justice Ministry to void wills offending the "sound judgment of the people"

◈ Decree providing for the compulsory sale of Jewish real estate

◈ Decree providing for the liquidation of Jewish real estate agencies, brokerage agencies, and marriage agencies catering to non-Jews

◈ Directive providing for the concentration of Jews in houses**July 6–15**

Evian Conference[190]: 31 countries refuse to accept Jews trying to escape Nazi Germany (with the exception of **Dominican Republic**[191]). Most find temporary refuge in Poland. See also **Bermuda Conference**[192]. **938**

Arab rioters rush into the Jewish Kiryat Shmuel neighborhood, killing 19 Jews, 11 of whom were children in the **1938 Tiberias massacre**[193]. **938**

Father **Charles E. Coughlin**[194], a Roman Catholic priest, starts antisemitic weekly radio broadcasts in the United States.

In his 1934 pageant play *The Rock*, **T.S. Eliot**[195] distances himself from Fascist movements of the thirties by caricaturing **Oswald Mosley**[196]'s Blackshirts, who 'firmly refuse/ To descend to palaver with anthropoid Jews'.[27][197] The "new evangels"[28][198] of totalitarianism are presented as antithetical to the spirit of Christianity. **938**

190. https://en.wikipedia.org/wiki/Evian_Conference

191. https://en.wikipedia.org/wiki/Dominican_Republic

192. https://en.wikipedia.org/wiki/Bermuda_Conference

193. https://en.wikipedia.org/wiki/1938_Tiberias_massacre

194. https://en.wikipedia.org/wiki/Charles_E._Coughlin

195. https://en.wikipedia.org/wiki/T.S._Eliot

196. https://en.wikipedia.org/wiki/Oswald_Mosley

Kristallnacht[199] (Night of The Broken Glass). In one night most German synagogues and hundreds of Jewish-owned German businesses are destroyed. Almost 100 Jews are killed, and 10,000 are sent to concentration camps.[35][200]

Racial legislation introduced in Italy. Anti Jewish economic legislation introduced in **Hungary**[201].

Der Giftpilz[202] is a children's book published by **Julius Streicher**[203] in 1938.[36][204] The title is German for "the **toadstool**[205]" or "the poisonous mushroom".[36][206] The book was intended as anti-Semitic propaganda. The text is by **Ernst Hiemer**[207], with illustrations by **Philipp Rupprecht**[208] (also known as *Fips*).

---

197. https://en.wikipedia.org/wiki/Timeline_of_antisemitism_in_the_20th_century#cite_note-27
198. https://en.wikipedia.org/wiki/Timeline_of_antisemitism_in_the_20th_century#cite_note-28
199. https://en.wikipedia.org/wiki/Kristallnacht
200. https://en.wikipedia.org/wiki/Timeline_of_antisemitism_in_the_20th_century#cite_note-35
201. https://en.wikipedia.org/wiki/Hungary
202. *https://en.wikipedia.org/wiki/Der_Giftpilz*
203. https://en.wikipedia.org/wiki/Julius_Streicher
204. https://en.wikipedia.org/wiki/Timeline_of_antisemitism_in_the_20th_century#cite_note-calvin-36
205. https://en.wikipedia.org/wiki/Toadstool
206. https://en.wikipedia.org/wiki/Timeline_of_antisemitism_in_the_20th_century#cite_note-calvin-36
207. https://en.wikipedia.org/wiki/Ernst_Hiemer

The "Voyage of the damned": **S.S. St. Louis**[209], carrying 907 Jewish refugees from Germany, is turned back by Canada, **Cuba**[210] and the US.[37][211] After they were denied entry to those places, the refugees were finally accepted in various European countries, including Belgium, the Netherlands, the UK, and France. Historians have estimated that approximately a quarter of them were murdered in death camps during World War II.

In this year **Ezra Pound**[212] returned to Italy from the States and began writing **antisemitic**[213] material for Italian newspapers. He wrote to **James Laughlin**[214] that **Roosevelt**[215] represented Jewry, and signed the letter with "**Heil Hitler**[216]".

1939

Linen from Ireland[217] is a 1939 German drama film that was part of an ongoing campaign of antisemitism in German cinema of the era, and it also attacked Britain with whom Germany was at war by the time of the film's release. **939**

---

208. https://en.wikipedia.org/wiki/Philipp_Rupprecht

209. https://en.wikipedia.org/wiki/MS_St._Louis

210. https://en.wikipedia.org/wiki/Cuba

211. https://en.wikipedia.org/wiki/Timeline_of_antisemitism_in_the_20th_century#cite_note-37

212. https://en.wikipedia.org/wiki/Ezra_Pound

213. https://en.wikipedia.org/wiki/Antisemitism

214. https://en.wikipedia.org/wiki/James_Laughlin

215. https://en.wikipedia.org/wiki/Franklin_D._Roosevelt

216. https://en.wikipedia.org/wiki/Heil_Hitler

217. *https://en.wikipedia.org/wiki/Linen_from_Ireland*

Robert and Bertram[218] is a 1939 German **musical**[219] **comedy film**[220]; it was the only anti-semitic **musical comedy**[221] released during the **Nazi**[222] era. **February**

The **Congress of the United States**[223] rejects the **Wagner-Rogers Bill**[224], an effort to admit 20,000 Jewish refugee children under the age of 14 from Nazi Germany.[38][225]**–1945**

The Holocaust[226]. About 6 million Jews, including about 1 million children, systematically killed by **Nazi Germany**[227] and other **Axis powers**[228]. See also **Holocaust denial**[229]. [edit[230]]

---

218. *https://en.wikipedia.org/wiki/Robert_and_Bertram_(1939_film)*
219. **https://en.wikipedia.org/wiki/Musical_film**
220. **https://en.wikipedia.org/wiki/Comedy_film**
221. **https://en.wikipedia.org/wiki/Musical_comedy**
222. **https://en.wikipedia.org/wiki/Nazi**
223. **https://en.wikipedia.org/wiki/Congress_of_the_United_States**
224. **https://en.wikipedia.org/wiki/Wagner-Rogers_Bill**
225. **https://en.wikipedia.org/wiki/Timeline_of_antisemitism_in_the_20th_century#cite_note-38**
226. https://en.wikipedia.org/wiki/The_Holocaust
227. **https://en.wikipedia.org/wiki/Nazi_Germany**
228. **https://en.wikipedia.org/wiki/Axis_powers**
229. **https://en.wikipedia.org/wiki/Holocaust_denial**
230. https://en.wikipedia.org/w/index.php?title=Timeline_of_antisemitism_in_the_20th_century&action=edit§ion=5

231

On 16 May 1940 the ***Administrasjonsrådet***[232] asked **Rikskommisariatet**[233] why radio receivers had been confiscated from Jews in Norway.[39][234] That *Administrasjonsrådet* thereafter "quietly" accepted[39][235] racial segregation between Norwegian citizens, has been claimed by **Tor Bomann-Larsen**[236]. Furthermore, he claimed that

231. https://en.wikipedia.org/wiki/File:German_officer_executes_Jewish_women_who_survived_a_mass_shooting_outside_the_Mizocz_ghetto,_14_October_1942.jpg

232. ***https://en.wikipedia.org/wiki/Administrasjonsr%C3%A5det***

233. **https://en.wikipedia.org/w/index.php?title=Rikskommisariatet&action=edit&redlink=1**

234. **https://en.wikipedia.org/wiki/Timeline_of_antisemitism_in_the_20th_century#cite_note-Folk_c0cb5f0fcf239ab3d9c1fcd31fff1efc__f_0bcef9c45bd8a48eda1b26eb0c61c869_C3_0bcef9c45bd8a48eda1b26eb0c61c869_B8rer_og_frifinnelse-39**

235. **https://en.wikipedia.org/wiki/Timeline_of_antisemitism_in_the_20th_century#cite_note-Folk_c0cb5f0fcf239ab3d9c1fcd31fff1efc__f_0bcef9c45bd8a48eda1b26eb0c61c869_C3_0bcef9c45bd8a48eda1b26eb0c61c869_B8rer_og_frifinnelse-39**

this segregation "created a **precedent**[237]." Two years later (with *NS-styret* in the ministries of Norway) Norwegian police **arrested citizens at the addresses**[238] where radios had previously been confiscated from Jews.[39][239]

1940

In the **Vichy regime**[240]: 10 July 1940 – **Pierre Laval**[241] induces Parliament to vote complete powers (constituent, legislative, executive and judicial) to Marshal **Philippe Pétain**[242] who becomes Head of state of the French State (État français). 21 July 1940 – Minister of Justice **Raphaël Alibert**[243] creates a board to review 500,000 naturalizations accorded since 1927. Withdrawal of nationality for 15,000 people, 40% of whom were Jews. July 1940 – The Germans expel more than 20,000 Alsace-Lorraine Jews to the southern zone. 27 September 1940 – Ordinance on the status of Jews in the Occupied Zone. A census of Jews ("the Tulard file") and obligatory sign indicating "Jew" on shops owned by Jews. 27 September 1940 – A Vichy law

236. https://en.wikipedia.org/wiki/Tor_Bomann-Larsen

237. https://en.wikipedia.org/wiki/Precedent

238. https://en.wikipedia.org/wiki/Jewish_deportees_from_Norway_during_World_War_II

239. https://en.wikipedia.org/wiki/Timeline_of_antisemitism_in_the_20th_century#cite_note-Folk_c0cb5f0fcf239ab3d9c1fcd31fff1efc__f_0bcef9c45bd8a48eda1b26eb0c61c869_C3_0bcef9c45bd8a48eda1b26eb0c61c869_B8rer_og_frifinnelse-39

240. https://en.wikipedia.org/wiki/Vichy_regime

241. https://en.wikipedia.org/wiki/Pierre_Laval

242. https://en.wikipedia.org/wiki/Philippe_P%C3%A9tain

243. https://en.wikipedia.org/wiki/Rapha%C3%ABl_Alibert

allows any foreigner "redundant to the French economy" to be interned among "groups of foreign workers". 3 October 1940 – first law on the status of Jews. French Jewish citizens are excluded from civil service, army, education, the press, radio and film. "Surplus" Jews are excluded from the professions. Article 9: This law is applicable to Algeria, to the colonies, protectorates and mandated territories. 4 October 1940 – prefects can detain foreigners of Jewish extraction in special camps or to assign residence. 7 October 1940 – repeal of the 18.71 billionémieux Decree; French nationality is removed from Jews from **Algeria**[244]. 7 October 1940 – Aryanization of businesses in the Occupied Zone.

1940

Jud Süß[245] is a 1940 **Nazi**[246] **propaganda film**[247] produced by Terra Filmkunst at the behest of **Joseph Goebbels**[248], and considered one of the most antisemitic films of all time.[40][249] The film has been characterized as "one of the most notorious and successful pieces of antisemitic film propaganda produced in Nazi Germany."[41][250] It was a great success in Germany, with some 20 million viewers. Although

244. https://en.wikipedia.org/wiki/Algeria

245. *https://en.wikipedia.org/wiki/Jud_S%C3%BC%C3%9F_(1940_film)*

246. https://en.wikipedia.org/wiki/Nazi_Germany

247. https://en.wikipedia.org/wiki/Propaganda_film

248. https://en.wikipedia.org/wiki/Joseph_Goebbels

249. https://en.wikipedia.org/wiki/Timeline_of_antisemitism_in_the_20th_century#cite_note-40

250. https://en.wikipedia.org/wiki/Timeline_of_antisemitism_in_the_20th_century#cite_note-CullCulbert2003-41

the film's budget of 2 million **Reichsmarks**[251] was considered high for films of that era, the box office receipts of 6.5 million Reichsmarks made it a financial success. **Heinrich Himmler**[252] urged members of the **SS**[253] and police to watch the movie.[42][254] **940**

The Rothschilds[255] is a 1940 German film directed by Erich Waschneck. It portrays the role of the **Rothschild family**[256] in the **Napoleonic Wars**[257]. The Jewish Rothschilds are depicted in a negative manner, consistent with the anti-Semitic policy of Nazi Germany.**1940**

Vom Bäumlein, das andere Blätter hat gewollt[258] is a short anti-Semitic propaganda cartoon produced in 1940 in the Nazi movie studio **Zeichenfilm GmbH**[259].**1940**

The Eternal Jew[260] (1940) is an antisemitic[43][261] **German Nazi**[262] **propaganda film**[263],[44][264] presented as a documentary.**1941**

251. https://en.wikipedia.org/wiki/Reichsmarks
252. https://en.wikipedia.org/wiki/Heinrich_Himmler
253. https://en.wikipedia.org/wiki/Schutzstaffel
254. https://en.wikipedia.org/wiki/Timeline_of_antisemitism_in_the_20th_century#cite_note-sz-42
255. *https://en.wikipedia.org/wiki/The_Rothschilds_(film)*
256. https://en.wikipedia.org/wiki/Rothschild_family
257. https://en.wikipedia.org/wiki/Napoleonic_Wars
258. *https://en.wikipedia.org/wiki/Vom_B%C3%A4umlein,_das_andere_Bl%C3%A4tter_hat_gewollt*
259. https://en.wikipedia.org/w/index.php?title=Zeichenfilm_GmbH&action=edit&redlink=1
260. *https://en.wikipedia.org/wiki/The_Eternal_Jew_(1940_film)*
261. https://en.wikipedia.org/wiki/Timeline_of_antisemitism_in_the_20th_century#cite_note-antisemitic-43
262. https://en.wikipedia.org/wiki/German_Nazi

The **Farhud**[265] pogrom in **Baghdad**[266] results in 780 Jews dead, over 1,000 wounded.[45][267]

Gabès pogrom[268] in **French Tunisia**[269] leaves 8 Jews dead and at least 20 wounded. **941**

Iași pogrom[270] in **Iași**[271] city was the incident where more than 13,266 Jews were killed by angry mobs of locals, and together with military personnel they exterminated about 1/3 of Jewish population in Romania.

Encouraged by the Nazis, Ukrainian militias and local mobs perpetrated the **Lviv pogroms**[272], killing around 6,000 Polish Jews.[46][273]

Some villagers in Jedwabne, Poland burned at least 340 local Jews alive.[47][274]

---

263. https://en.wikipedia.org/wiki/Propaganda_film

264. https://en.wikipedia.org/wiki/Timeline_of_antisemitism_in_the_20th_century#cite_note-Propaganda_film-44

265. https://en.wikipedia.org/wiki/Farhud

266. https://en.wikipedia.org/wiki/Baghdad

267. https://en.wikipedia.org/wiki/Timeline_of_antisemitism_in_the_20th_century#cite_note-45

268. https://en.wikipedia.org/wiki/Gab%C3%A8s_pogrom

269. https://en.wikipedia.org/wiki/French_Tunisia

270. https://en.wikipedia.org/wiki/Ia%C8%99i_pogrom

271. https://en.wikipedia.org/wiki/Ia%C8%99i

272. https://en.wikipedia.org/wiki/Lviv_pogroms_(1941)

273. https://en.wikipedia.org/wiki/Timeline_of_antisemitism_in_the_20th_century#cite_note-46

1941

Nazis and their collaborators shot to death 33,771 Jews at **Babi Yar**[275] over the course of two days.[48][276]

1941

German forces and Latvian collaborators killed around 5,000 Jews in the **Liepāja massacres**[277].

1941

In a speech at an America First rally at the **Des Moines Coliseum**[278] on 11 September 1941, "Who Are the War Agitators?", **Charles Lindbergh**[279] warned of the Jewish people's "large ownership and influence in our motion pictures, our press, our radio, and our government"[49][280] and claimed the three groups "pressing this country toward war [are] the British, the Jewish, and the Roosevelt Administration",[50][281] and said of Jewish groups,

---

274. https://en.wikipedia.org/wiki/Timeline_of_antisemitism_in_the_20th_century#cite_note-47

275. https://en.wikipedia.org/wiki/Babi_Yar

276. https://en.wikipedia.org/wiki/Timeline_of_antisemitism_in_the_20th_century#cite_note-48

277. https://en.wikipedia.org/wiki/Liep%C4%81ja_massacres

278. https://en.wikipedia.org/wiki/Des_Moines_Coliseum

279. https://en.wikipedia.org/wiki/Charles_Lindbergh

280. https://en.wikipedia.org/wiki/Timeline_of_antisemitism_in_the_20th_century#cite_note-Des_Moines-49

1941

Collaboration of the **Vichy regime**[282] with the **Holocaust**[283]: 29 March 1941: creation of the **Commissariat-General for Jewish Affairs**[284] (CGQJ), with Xavier Vallat as the first commissioner. 11 May 1941 – Creation of the French Institute for Jewish Affairs, an anti-Semitic propaganda agency, financed by the nazis (Theodor Dannecker) and directed by French antisemitic agitators Paul Sézille (fr), René Gérard (fr) and others. 14 May 1941 – the Billet Vert roundup (fr) organized by the Prefecture of Police with the agreement of the general delegation of the French government in the occupied zone and upon demand by the occupying authorities: 3,747 Jewish foreigners, (out of 6,494 summoned by the prefecture) were crammed into the Pithiviers and Beaune-la-Rolande internment camps under French administration. 2 June 1941 – second law concerning Jews. Compared to the first one, an increasingly stringent definition of who is a Jew, additional professional work restrictions, quotas in University (3%) and the liberal professions (2%). Jews were obligated to take part in a census in the Zone libre. Article 11 of the Statute: "This law is applicable to Algeria, the colonies, protectorates and territories under mandate. This law authorizes prefects to perform administrative detention of Jews of French nationality." 21 July 1941 – Aryanization of Jewish companies in the Zone libre. August 1941: Occupied zone: internment of 3,200 foreign and 1,000 French Jews in various camps including Drancy. December 1941 – Occupied zone: 740 French Jews, members of the liberal and intellectual professions, interned in Compiègne.**1942**

---

281. https://en.wikipedia.org/wiki/Timeline_of_antisemitism_in_the_20th_century#cite_note-50

282. https://en.wikipedia.org/wiki/Vichy_regime

283. https://en.wikipedia.org/wiki/Holocaust

284. https://en.wikipedia.org/wiki/Commissariat-General_for_Jewish_Affairs

In January the **Wannsee Conference**[285] takes place in Berlin. Nazi officials define the practical arrangements for the "Final Solution", that is to say, the complete extermination of European Jewry, including children. **942**

The **Antisemitic Exhibition in Zagreb**[286] took place in the **Art Pavilion**[287] in **Zagreb**[288], the capital city of the **Independent State of Croatia**[289] (NDH), in May 1942. According to its organizers, the exhibition sought to expose the "destructive and exploitative work of **Croatia**[290]'s Jews prior to 1941." **942**

Collaboration of the **Vichy regime**[291] with the **Holocaust**[292]: 27 March 1942 – The first convoy of Jewish deportees leaves Compiègne (Frontstalag 122) towards an extermination camp. 20 May 1942 – Occupied zone: Compulsory wearing of yellow Jewish star badge. (effective 7 June). 2 July 1942 – Oberg-Bousquet agreement for collaboration between French and German police, in the presence of **Reinhard Heydrich**[293], **Heinrich Himmler**[294]'s deputy. 16–17 July 1942 – **Roundup of the Vel d'Hiv**[295]: arrest of 13,152 "stateless" Jews (3,031 men, 5,802 women and 4,051 children). 19 July 1942 – failed Roundup of Nancy (fr), after Jews were warned overnight to flee by Nancy Police Commissioner for Foreign Affairs Édouard Vigneron.

---

285. https://en.wikipedia.org/wiki/Wannsee_Conference
286. https://en.wikipedia.org/wiki/Antisemitic_Exhibition_in_Zagreb
287. https://en.wikipedia.org/wiki/Art_Pavilion_in_Zagreb
288. https://en.wikipedia.org/wiki/Zagreb
289. https://en.wikipedia.org/wiki/Independent_State_of_Croatia
290. https://en.wikipedia.org/wiki/Croatia
291. https://en.wikipedia.org/wiki/Vichy_regime
292. https://en.wikipedia.org/wiki/Holocaust
293. https://en.wikipedia.org/wiki/Reinhard_Heydrich
294. https://en.wikipedia.org/wiki/Heinrich_Himmler
295. https://en.wikipedia.org/wiki/Vel%27_d%27Hiv_Roundup

26–28 August 1942 Zone libre – series of roundups resulting in the deportation of 7,000 people.**1943**

Vienna 1910[296] is a 1943 German biographical film directed by Emerich Walter Emo and starring Rudolf Forster, Heinrich George and Lil Dagover. It is based on the life of Mayor of Vienna Karl Lueger. Its antisemitic content led to it being banned by the Allied Occupation forces following World War II.

Forces occultes[297] is a French film of 1943 that virulently denounces Jews, **Freemasonry**[298], and parliamentarianism as part of the **Vichy regime**[299]'s drive against them and seeks to prove a Jewish-Masonic plot.

Collaboration of the **Vichy regime**[300] with the **Holocaust**[301]: January 1943 – **Roundup of Marseille**[302]: destruction of the Old Port and roundups by French authorities. Nearly 2,000 Marseilles Jews arrested and deported. Le Petit Marseillais of 30 January 1943 wrote: "Note that the evacuation operations in the Northern district of the Old Port were carried out exclusively by French police and that no incidents were reported. The Opera district, where many Sephardic families lived, is emptied of its inhabitants. February 1943 – Lyon raid on the premises of the **Union générale des israélites de France**[303] (UGIF, General Organization of Jews in France). September 8, 1943 – surrender of Italy leading to the Allied occupation of Italian-occupied

---

296. *https://en.wikipedia.org/wiki/Vienna_1910*

297. *https://en.wikipedia.org/wiki/Forces_occultes*

298. https://en.wikipedia.org/wiki/Freemasonry

299. https://en.wikipedia.org/wiki/Vichy_regime

300. https://en.wikipedia.org/wiki/Vichy_regime

301. https://en.wikipedia.org/wiki/Holocaust

302. https://en.wikipedia.org/wiki/Roundup_of_Marseille

303. https://en.wikipedia.org/wiki/Union_g%C3%A9n%C3%A9rale_des_isra%C3%A9lites_de_France

France hitherto spared the roundups. April 1943 – Nîmes and Avignon roundups. September 1943 – roundups of Nice and surrounding area."

1943

The **Bermuda Conference**[304] was an international conference between the United Kingdom and the United States held from 19 April 1943, through 30 April 1943, at **Hamilton, Bermuda**[305]. The topic of discussion was the question of Jewish **refugees**[306] who had been liberated by **Allied forces**[307] and those who still remained in **Nazi**[308]-occupied Europe. The only agreement made was that the war must be won against the Nazis. US immigration quotas were not raised nor was the British prohibition on Jewish refugees seeking refuge in the **British Mandate of Palestine**[309] lifted.

1944

Collaboration of the **Vichy regime**[310] with the **Holocaust**[311]: February 1944 – roundups of Grenoble and Isère. 15 August 1944 – last deportation convoy from Clermont-Ferrand.

1945

The **1945 Tripoli pogrom**[312] was a violent massacre of the **Jewish population of Tripoli**[313] by Muslim rioters. After days of violence 140+ Jews were dead and hundreds were injured. In the aftermath 4,000 Jews were left homeless and thousands were reduced to poverty.

---

304. https://en.wikipedia.org/wiki/Bermuda_Conference
305. https://en.wikipedia.org/wiki/Hamilton,_Bermuda
306. https://en.wikipedia.org/wiki/Refugee
307. https://en.wikipedia.org/wiki/Allies_of_World_War_II
308. https://en.wikipedia.org/wiki/Nazi_Germany
309. https://en.wikipedia.org/wiki/Mandatory_Palestine
310. https://en.wikipedia.org/wiki/Vichy_regime
311. https://en.wikipedia.org/wiki/Holocaust
312. https://en.wikipedia.org/wiki/1945_Tripoli_pogrom
313. https://en.wikipedia.org/wiki/Libyan_Jews

9 Synagogues were destroyed, along with thousands of Jewish homes and businesses.

1945

The **1945 Anti-Jewish riots in Egypt**[314] started as an **anti-Zionist**[315] demonstration, but it ended with the killing of 5 **Egyptian Zionists**[316] by a Muslim mob and over 300 other Jews were injured.

1945

Bess Myerson[317] was the first Jewish-American and the first **Miss New York**[318][51][319] (competing as Miss New York City, a competition organized by a local radio station[52][320]) to win the Miss America Pageant as Miss America 1945.[52][321][53][322][54][323][55][324][56][325] As

314. https://en.wikipedia.org/wiki/1945_Anti-Jewish_riots_in_Egypt
315. https://en.wikipedia.org/wiki/Anti-Zionist
316. https://en.wikipedia.org/wiki/Egyptian_Jews
317. https://en.wikipedia.org/wiki/Bess_Myerson
318. https://en.wikipedia.org/wiki/Miss_New_York
319. https://en.wikipedia.org/wiki/Timeline_of_antisemitism_in_the_20th_century#cite_note-mabio-51
320. https://en.wikipedia.org/wiki/Timeline_of_antisemitism_in_the_20th_century#cite_note-latobit-52
321. https://en.wikipedia.org/wiki/Timeline_of_antisemitism_in_the_20th_century#cite_note-latobit-52
322. https://en.wikipedia.org/wiki/Timeline_of_antisemitism_in_the_20th_century#cite_note-americanexperiencetranscript-53
323. https://en.wikipedia.org/wiki/Timeline_of_antisemitism_in_the_20th_century#cite_note-nymagbess-54

the only Jewish contestant, Myerson was encouraged by the pageant directors to change her name to "Bess Meredith"[54][326] or "Beth Merrick"[53][327] but she refused.[53][328][54][329] After winning the title (and as a Jewish Miss America), Myerson received few endorsements[52][330][53][331][54][332][55][333][56][334] and later recalled that "I couldn't even stay in certain hotels [...] there would be signs that

324. https://en.wikipedia.org/wiki/Timeline_of_antisemitism_in_the_20th_century#cite_note-nytmyobit-55
325. https://en.wikipedia.org/wiki/Timeline_of_antisemitism_in_the_20th_century#cite_note-wsjobitbm-56
326. https://en.wikipedia.org/wiki/Timeline_of_antisemitism_in_the_20th_century#cite_note-nymagbess-54
327. https://en.wikipedia.org/wiki/Timeline_of_antisemitism_in_the_20th_century#cite_note-americanexperiencetranscript-53
328. https://en.wikipedia.org/wiki/Timeline_of_antisemitism_in_the_20th_century#cite_note-americanexperiencetranscript-53
329. https://en.wikipedia.org/wiki/Timeline_of_antisemitism_in_the_20th_century#cite_note-nymagbess-54
330. https://en.wikipedia.org/wiki/Timeline_of_antisemitism_in_the_20th_century#cite_note-latobit-52
331. https://en.wikipedia.org/wiki/Timeline_of_antisemitism_in_the_20th_century#cite_note-americanexperiencetranscript-53
332. https://en.wikipedia.org/wiki/Timeline_of_antisemitism_in_the_20th_century#cite_note-nymagbess-54

read no coloreds, no Jews, no dogs. I felt so rejected. Here I was chosen to represent American womanhood and then America treated me like this."[54][335] She thus cut short her Miss America tour and instead traveled with the **Anti-Defamation League**[336]. In this capacity, she spoke against discrimination in a talk entitled, "You Can't Be Beautiful and Hate."[52][337][53][338][54][339][55][340][56][341]

1945

The **Kraków pogrom**[342] was a post-WW2 pogrom, resulting in the death of **Auschwitz**[343] survivor **Róża Berger**[344].

---

333. https://en.wikipedia.org/wiki/Timeline_of_antisemitism_in_the_20th_century#cite_note-nytmyobit-55
334. https://en.wikipedia.org/wiki/Timeline_of_antisemitism_in_the_20th_century#cite_note-wsjobitbm-56
335. https://en.wikipedia.org/wiki/Timeline_of_antisemitism_in_the_20th_century#cite_note-nymagbess-54
336. https://en.wikipedia.org/wiki/Anti-Defamation_League
337. https://en.wikipedia.org/wiki/Timeline_of_antisemitism_in_the_20th_century#cite_note-latobit-52
338. https://en.wikipedia.org/wiki/Timeline_of_antisemitism_in_the_20th_century#cite_note-americanexperiencetranscript-53
339. https://en.wikipedia.org/wiki/Timeline_of_antisemitism_in_the_20th_century#cite_note-nymagbess-54
340. https://en.wikipedia.org/wiki/Timeline_of_antisemitism_in_the_20th_century#cite_note-nytmyobit-55
341. https://en.wikipedia.org/wiki/Timeline_of_antisemitism_in_the_20th_century#cite_note-wsjobitbm-56

1946

The **Kielce pogrom**[345]. 40 Jews were massacred and 80 other Jews were wounded out of about 200 who had returned home after **World War II**[346] had ended. 2 non-Jewish Poles were also killed. Controversy was caused by **August Hlond**[347]'s reaction to the **Kielce pogrom**[348]. While condemning murders, Hlond denied the racist nature of this crime.[57][349][58][350] He saw the pogrom as a reaction against Jewish bureaucrats serving the Communist regime.[58][351] This position was echoed by **Cardinal Sapieha**[352], who was reported to have said that the Jews brought it on

---

342. https://en.wikipedia.org/wiki/Krak%C3%B3w_pogrom

343. https://en.wikipedia.org/wiki/Auschwitz

344. https://en.wikipedia.org/wiki/R%C3%B3%C5%BCa_Berger

345. https://en.wikipedia.org/wiki/Kielce_pogrom

346. https://en.wikipedia.org/wiki/World_War_II

347. https://en.wikipedia.org/wiki/August_Hlond

348. https://en.wikipedia.org/wiki/Kielce_pogrom

349. https://en.wikipedia.org/wiki/Timeline_of_antisemitism_in_the_20th_century#cite_note-Kent-57

350. https://en.wikipedia.org/wiki/Timeline_of_antisemitism_in_the_20th_century#cite_note-Phayer-58

351. https://en.wikipedia.org/wiki/Timeline_of_antisemitism_in_the_20th_century#cite_note-Phayer-58

352. https://en.wikipedia.org/wiki/Cardinal_Sapieha

[353]

General **Eisenhower**[354] inspecting prisoners' corpses at Dachau.

On 16 May 1940 the ***Administrasjonsrådet***[355] asked **Rikskommisariatet**[356] why radio receivers had been confiscated from Jews in Norway.[39][357] That *Administrasjonsrådet* thereafter "quietly" accepted[39][358] racial segregation between Norwegian citizens, has

---

353. https://en.wikipedia.org/wiki/File:Ohrdruf_Eisenhower_04649.jpg

354. **https://en.wikipedia.org/wiki/Dwight_Eisenhower**

355. ***https://en.wikipedia.org/wiki/Administrasjonsr%C3%A5det***

356. **https://en.wikipedia.org/w/ index.php?title=Rikskommisariatet&action=edit&redlink=1**

357. **https://en.wikipedia.org/wiki/ Timeline_of_antisemitism_in_the_20th_century#cite_note-Folk_c0cb5f0fcf 239ab3d9c1fcd31fff1efc__f_0bcef9c45bd8a48eda1b26eb0c61c869_C3_0bce f9c45bd8a48eda1b26eb0c61c869_B8rer_og_frifinnelse-39**

358. **https://en.wikipedia.org/wiki/ Timeline_of_antisemitism_in_the_20th_century#cite_note-Folk_c0cb5f0fcf**

been claimed by **Tor Bomann-Larsen**[359]. Furthermore, he claimed that this segregation "created a **precedent**[360]." Two years later (with *NS-styret* in the ministries of Norway) Norwegian police **arrested citizens at the addresses**[361] where radios had previously been confiscated from Jews.[39][362]

1940

In the **Vichy regime**[363]: 10 July 1940 – **Pierre Laval**[364] induces Parliament to vote complete powers (constituent, legislative, executive and judicial) to Marshal **Philippe Pétain**[365] who becomes Head of state of the French State (État français). 21 July 1940 – Minister of Justice **Raphaël Alibert**[366] creates a board to review 500,000 naturalizations accorded since 1927. Withdrawal of nationality for 15,000 people, 40% of whom were Jews. July 1940 – The Germans expel more than 20,000 Alsace-Lorraine Jews to the southern zone. 27

239ab3d9c1fcd31fff1efc__f_0bcef9c45bd8a48eda1b26eb0c61c869_C3_0bce f9c45bd8a48eda1b26eb0c61c869_B8rer_og_frifinnelse-39

359. https://en.wikipedia.org/wiki/Tor_Bomann-Larsen

360. https://en.wikipedia.org/wiki/Precedent

361. https://en.wikipedia.org/wiki/Jewish_deportees_from_Norway_during_World_War_II

362. https://en.wikipedia.org/wiki/Timeline_of_antisemitism_in_the_20th_century#cite_note-Folk_c0cb5f0fcf239ab3d9c1fcd31fff1efc__f_0bcef9c45bd8a48eda1b26eb0c61c869_C3_0bcef9c45bd8a48eda1b26eb0c61c869_B8rer_og_frifinnelse-39

363. https://en.wikipedia.org/wiki/Vichy_regime

364. https://en.wikipedia.org/wiki/Pierre_Laval

365. https://en.wikipedia.org/wiki/Philippe_P%C3%A9tain

366. https://en.wikipedia.org/wiki/Rapha%C3%ABl_Alibert

September 1940 – Ordinance on the status of Jews in the Occupied Zone. A census of Jews ("the Tulard file") and obligatory sign indicating "Jew" on shops owned by Jews. 27 September 1940 – A Vichy law allows any foreigner "redundant to the French economy" to be interned among "groups of foreign workers". 3 October 1940 – first law on the status of Jews. French Jewish citizens are excluded from civil service, army, education, the press, radio and film. "Surplus" Jews are excluded from the professions. Article 9: This law is applicable to Algeria, to the colonies, protectorates and mandated territories. 4 October 1940 – prefects can detain foreigners of Jewish extraction in special camps or to assign residence. 7 October 1940 – repeal of the 18.71 billionémieux Decree; French nationality is removed from Jews from **Algeria**[367]. 7 October 1940 – Aryanization of businesses in the Occupied Zone.

1940

Jud Süß[368] is a 1940 **Nazi**[369] **propaganda film**[370] produced by Terra Filmkunst at the behest of **Joseph Goebbels**[371], and considered one of the most antisemitic films of all time.[40][372] The film has been characterized as "one of the most notorious and successful pieces of antisemitic film propaganda produced in Nazi Germany."[41][373] It was a great success in Germany, with some 20 million viewers. Although the film's budget of 2 million **Reichsmarks**[374] was considered high for

367. https://en.wikipedia.org/wiki/Algeria

368. *https://en.wikipedia.org/wiki/Jud_S%C3%BC%C3%9F_(1940_film)*

369. https://en.wikipedia.org/wiki/Nazi_Germany

370. https://en.wikipedia.org/wiki/Propaganda_film

371. https://en.wikipedia.org/wiki/Joseph_Goebbels

372. https://en.wikipedia.org/wiki/Timeline_of_antisemitism_in_the_20th_century#cite_note-40

films of that era, the box office receipts of 6.5 million Reichsmarks made it a financial success. **Heinrich Himmler**[375] urged members of the **SS**[376] and police to watch the movie.[42][377]

1940

The Rothschilds[378] is a 1940 German film directed by Erich Waschneck. It portrays the role of the **Rothschild family**[379] in the **Napoleonic Wars**[380]. The Jewish Rothschilds are depicted in a negative manner, consistent with the anti-Semitic policy of Nazi Germany.

1940

Vom Bäumlein, das andere Blätter hat gewollt[381] is a short anti-Semitic propaganda cartoon produced in 1940 in the Nazi movie studio **Zeichenfilm GmbH**[382].

---

373. https://en.wikipedia.org/wiki/Timeline_of_antisemitism_in_the_20th_century#cite_note-CullCulbert2003-41

374. https://en.wikipedia.org/wiki/Reichsmarks

375. https://en.wikipedia.org/wiki/Heinrich_Himmler

376. https://en.wikipedia.org/wiki/Schutzstaffel

377. https://en.wikipedia.org/wiki/Timeline_of_antisemitism_in_the_20th_century#cite_note-sz-42

378. *https://en.wikipedia.org/wiki/The_Rothschilds_(film)*

379. https://en.wikipedia.org/wiki/Rothschild_family

380. https://en.wikipedia.org/wiki/Napoleonic_Wars

381. *https://en.wikipedia.org/wiki/Vom_B%C3%A4umlein,_das_andere_Bl%C3%A4tter_hat_gewollt*

382. https://en.wikipedia.org/w/index.php?title=Zeichenfilm_GmbH&action=edit&redlink=1

1940

The Eternal Jew[383] (1940) is an antisemitic[43][384] **German Nazi**[385] **propaganda film**[386],[44][387] presented as a documentary.

1941

The **Farhud**[388] pogrom in **Baghdad**[389] results in 780 Jews dead, over 1,000 wounded.[45][390]

1941

Gabès pogrom[391] in **French Tunisia**[392] leaves 8 Jews dead and at least 20 wounded.

1941

---

383. *https://en.wikipedia.org/wiki/The_Eternal_Jew_(1940_film)*

384. https://en.wikipedia.org/wiki/Timeline_of_antisemitism_in_the_20th_century#cite_note-antisemitic-43

385. https://en.wikipedia.org/wiki/German_Nazi

386. https://en.wikipedia.org/wiki/Propaganda_film

387. https://en.wikipedia.org/wiki/Timeline_of_antisemitism_in_the_20th_century#cite_note-Propaganda_film-44

388. https://en.wikipedia.org/wiki/Farhud

389. https://en.wikipedia.org/wiki/Baghdad

390. https://en.wikipedia.org/wiki/Timeline_of_antisemitism_in_the_20th_century#cite_note-45

391. https://en.wikipedia.org/wiki/Gab%C3%A8s_pogrom

392. https://en.wikipedia.org/wiki/French_Tunisia

Iași pogrom[393] in **Iași**[394] city was the incident where more than 13,266 Jews were killed by angry mobs of locals, and together with military personnel they exterminated about 1/3 of Jewish population in Romania.

1941

Encouraged by the Nazis, Ukrainian militias and local mobs perpetrated the **Lviv pogroms**[395], killing around 6,000 Polish Jews.[46][396]

1941

Some villagers in Jedwabne, Poland burned at least 340 local Jews alive.[47][397]

1941

Nazis and their collaborators shot to death 33,771 Jews at **Babi Yar**[398] over the course of two days.[48][399]

---

393. https://en.wikipedia.org/wiki/Ia%C8%99i_pogrom
394. https://en.wikipedia.org/wiki/Ia%C8%99i
395. https://en.wikipedia.org/wiki/Lviv_pogroms_(1941)
396. https://en.wikipedia.org/wiki/Timeline_of_antisemitism_in_the_20th_century#cite_note-46
397. https://en.wikipedia.org/wiki/Timeline_of_antisemitism_in_the_20th_century#cite_note-47
398. https://en.wikipedia.org/wiki/Babi_Yar
399. https://en.wikipedia.org/wiki/Timeline_of_antisemitism_in_the_20th_century#cite_note-48

1941

German forces and Latvian collaborators killed around 5,000 Jews in the **Liepāja massacres**[400].

1941

In a speech at an America First rally at the **Des Moines Coliseum**[401] on 11 September 1941, "Who Are the War Agitators?", **Charles Lindbergh**[402] warned of the Jewish people's "large ownership and influence in our motion pictures, our press, our radio, and our government"**[49]**[403] and claimed the three groups "pressing this country toward war [are] the British, the Jewish, and the Roosevelt Administration",**[50]**[404] and said of Jewish groups,

1941

Collaboration of the **Vichy regime**[405] with the **Holocaust**[406]: 29 March 1941: creation of the **Commissariat-General for Jewish Affairs**[407] (CGQJ), with Xavier Vallat as the first commissioner. 11

---

400. https://en.wikipedia.org/wiki/Liep%C4%81ja_massacres
401. https://en.wikipedia.org/wiki/Des_Moines_Coliseum
402. https://en.wikipedia.org/wiki/Charles_Lindbergh
403. https://en.wikipedia.org/wiki/Timeline_of_antisemitism_in_the_20th_century#cite_note-Des_Moines-49
404. https://en.wikipedia.org/wiki/Timeline_of_antisemitism_in_the_20th_century#cite_note-50
405. https://en.wikipedia.org/wiki/Vichy_regime
406. https://en.wikipedia.org/wiki/Holocaust
407. https://en.wikipedia.org/wiki/Commissariat-General_for_Jewish_Affairs

May 1941 – Creation of the French Institute for Jewish Affairs, an anti-Semitic propaganda agency, financed by the nazis (Theodor Dannecker) and directed by French antisemitic agitators Paul Sézille (fr), René Gérard (fr) and others. 14 May 1941 – the Billet Vert roundup (fr) organized by the Prefecture of Police with the agreement of the general delegation of the French government in the occupied zone and upon demand by the occupying authorities: 3,747 Jewish foreigners, (out of 6,494 summoned by the prefecture) were crammed into the Pithiviers and Beaune-la-Rolande internment camps under French administration. 2 June 1941 – second law concerning Jews. Compared to the first one, an increasingly stringent definition of who is a Jew, additional professional work restrictions, quotas in University (3%) and the liberal professions (2%). Jews were obligated to take part in a census in the Zone libre. Article 11 of the Statute: "This law is applicable to Algeria, the colonies, protectorates and territories under mandate. This law authorizes prefects to perform administrative detention of Jews of French nationality." 21 July 1941 – Aryanization of Jewish companies in the Zone libre. August 1941: Occupied zone: internment of 3,200 foreign and 1,000 French Jews in various camps including Drancy. December 1941 – Occupied zone: 740 French Jews, members of the liberal and intellectual professions, interned in Compiègne.

1942

In January the **Wannsee Conference**[408] takes place in Berlin. Nazi officials define the practical arrangements for the "Final Solution", that is to say, the complete extermination of European Jewry, including children.

1942

408. https://en.wikipedia.org/wiki/Wannsee_Conference

The **Antisemitic Exhibition in Zagreb**[409] took place in the **Art Pavilion**[410] in **Zagreb**[411], the capital city of the **Independent State of Croatia**[412] (NDH), in May 1942. According to its organizers, the exhibition sought to expose the "destructive and exploitative work of **Croatia**[413]'s Jews prior to 1941."

1942

Collaboration of the **Vichy regime**[414] with the **Holocaust**[415]: 27 March 1942 – The first convoy of Jewish deportees leaves Compiègne (Frontstalag 122) towards an extermination camp. 20 May 1942 – Occupied zone: Compulsory wearing of yellow Jewish star badge. (effective 7 June). 2 July 1942 – Oberg-Bousquet agreement for collaboration between French and German police, in the presence of **Reinhard Heydrich**[416], **Heinrich Himmler**[417]'s deputy. 16–17 July 1942 – **Roundup of the Vel d'Hiv**[418]: arrest of 13,152 "stateless" Jews (3,031 men, 5,802 women and 4,051 children). 19 July 1942 – failed Roundup of Nancy (fr), after Jews were warned overnight to flee by Nancy Police Commissioner for Foreign Affairs Édouard Vigneron. 26–28 August 1942 Zone libre – series of roundups resulting in the deportation of 7,000 people.

1943

409. https://en.wikipedia.org/wiki/Antisemitic_Exhibition_in_Zagreb
410. https://en.wikipedia.org/wiki/Art_Pavilion_in_Zagreb
411. https://en.wikipedia.org/wiki/Zagreb
412. https://en.wikipedia.org/wiki/Independent_State_of_Croatia
413. https://en.wikipedia.org/wiki/Croatia
414. https://en.wikipedia.org/wiki/Vichy_regime
415. https://en.wikipedia.org/wiki/Holocaust
416. https://en.wikipedia.org/wiki/Reinhard_Heydrich
417. https://en.wikipedia.org/wiki/Heinrich_Himmler
418. https://en.wikipedia.org/wiki/Vel%27_d%27Hiv_Roundup

Vienna 1910[419] is a 1943 German biographical film directed by Emerich Walter Emo and starring Rudolf Forster, Heinrich George and Lil Dagover. It is based on the life of Mayor of Vienna Karl Lueger. Its antisemitic content led to it being banned by the Allied Occupation forces following World War II.

1943

Forces occultes[420] is a French film of 1943 that virulently denounces Jews, **Freemasonry**[421], and parliamentarianism as part of the **Vichy regime**[422]'s drive against them and seeks to prove a Jewish-Masonic plot.

1943

Collaboration of the **Vichy regime**[423] with the **Holocaust**[424]: January 1943 – **Roundup of Marseille**[425]: destruction of the Old Port and roundups by French authorities. Nearly 2,000 Marseilles Jews arrested and deported. Le Petit Marseillais of 30 January 1943 wrote: "Note that the evacuation operations in the Northern district of the Old Port were carried out exclusively by French police and that no incidents were reported. The Opera district, where many Sephardic families lived, is emptied of its inhabitants. February 1943 – Lyon raid on the premises of the **Union générale des israélites de France**[426] (UGIF, General Organization of Jews in France). September 8, 1943 – surrender of Italy leading to the Allied occupation of Italian-occupied

---

419. https://en.wikipedia.org/wiki/Vienna_1910

420. https://en.wikipedia.org/wiki/Forces_occultes

421. https://en.wikipedia.org/wiki/Freemasonry

422. https://en.wikipedia.org/wiki/Vichy_regime

423. https://en.wikipedia.org/wiki/Vichy_regime

424. https://en.wikipedia.org/wiki/Holocaust

425. https://en.wikipedia.org/wiki/Roundup_of_Marseille

426. https://en.wikipedia.org/wiki/
Union_g%C3%A9n%C3%A9rale_des_isra%C3%A9lites_de_France

France hitherto spared the roundups. April 1943 – Nîmes and Avignon roundups. September 1943 – roundups of Nice and surrounding area."

1943

The **Bermuda Conference**[427] was an international conference between the United Kingdom and the United States held from 19 April 1943, through 30 April 1943, at **Hamilton, Bermuda**[428]. The topic of discussion was the question of Jewish **refugees**[429] who had been liberated by **Allied forces**[430] and those who still remained in **Nazi**[431]-occupied Europe. The only agreement made was that the war must be won against the Nazis. US immigration quotas were not raised nor was the British prohibition on Jewish refugees seeking refuge in the **British Mandate of Palestine**[432] lifted.

1944

Collaboration of the **Vichy regime**[433] with the **Holocaust**[434]: February 1944 – roundups of Grenoble and Isère. 15 August 1944 – last deportation convoy from Clermont-Ferrand.

1945

The **1945 Tripoli pogrom**[435] was a violent massacre of the **Jewish population of Tripoli**[436] by Muslim rioters. After days of violence 140+ Jews were dead and hundreds were injured. In the aftermath 4,000 Jews were left homeless and thousands were reduced to poverty.

---

427. https://en.wikipedia.org/wiki/Bermuda_Conference
428. https://en.wikipedia.org/wiki/Hamilton,_Bermuda
429. https://en.wikipedia.org/wiki/Refugee
430. https://en.wikipedia.org/wiki/Allies_of_World_War_II
431. https://en.wikipedia.org/wiki/Nazi_Germany
432. https://en.wikipedia.org/wiki/Mandatory_Palestine
433. https://en.wikipedia.org/wiki/Vichy_regime
434. https://en.wikipedia.org/wiki/Holocaust
435. https://en.wikipedia.org/wiki/1945_Tripoli_pogrom
436. https://en.wikipedia.org/wiki/Libyan_Jews

9 Synagogues were destroyed, along with thousands of Jewish homes and businesses.

1945

The **1945 Anti-Jewish riots in Egypt**[437] started as an **anti-Zionist**[438] demonstration, but it ended with the killing of 5 **Egyptian Zionists**[439] by a Muslim mob and over 300 other Jews were injured.

1945

Bess Myerson[440] was the first Jewish-American and the first **Miss New York**[441][51][442] (competing as Miss New York City, a competition organized by a local radio station[52][443]) to win the Miss America Pageant as Miss America 1945.[52][444][53][445][54][446][55][447][56][448] As

437. https://en.wikipedia.org/wiki/1945_Anti-Jewish_riots_in_Egypt

438. https://en.wikipedia.org/wiki/Anti-Zionist

439. https://en.wikipedia.org/wiki/Egyptian_Jews

440. https://en.wikipedia.org/wiki/Bess_Myerson

441. https://en.wikipedia.org/wiki/Miss_New_York

442. https://en.wikipedia.org/wiki/Timeline_of_antisemitism_in_the_20th_century#cite_note-mabio-51

443. https://en.wikipedia.org/wiki/Timeline_of_antisemitism_in_the_20th_century#cite_note-latobit-52

444. https://en.wikipedia.org/wiki/Timeline_of_antisemitism_in_the_20th_century#cite_note-latobit-52

445. https://en.wikipedia.org/wiki/Timeline_of_antisemitism_in_the_20th_century#cite_note-americanexperiencetranscript-53

446. https://en.wikipedia.org/wiki/Timeline_of_antisemitism_in_the_20th_century#cite_note-nymagbess-54

the only Jewish contestant, Myerson was encouraged by the pageant directors to change her name to "Bess Meredith"[54][449] or "Beth Merrick"[53][450] but she refused.[53][451][54][452] After winning the title (and as a Jewish Miss America), Myerson received few endorsements[52][453][53][454][54][455][55][456][56][457] and later recalled that "I couldn't even stay in certain hotels [...] there would be signs that

447. https://en.wikipedia.org/wiki/Timeline_of_antisemitism_in_the_20th_century#cite_note-nytmyobit-55
448. https://en.wikipedia.org/wiki/Timeline_of_antisemitism_in_the_20th_century#cite_note-wsjobitbm-56
449. https://en.wikipedia.org/wiki/Timeline_of_antisemitism_in_the_20th_century#cite_note-nymagbess-54
450. https://en.wikipedia.org/wiki/Timeline_of_antisemitism_in_the_20th_century#cite_note-americanexperiencetranscript-53
451. https://en.wikipedia.org/wiki/Timeline_of_antisemitism_in_the_20th_century#cite_note-americanexperiencetranscript-53
452. https://en.wikipedia.org/wiki/Timeline_of_antisemitism_in_the_20th_century#cite_note-nymagbess-54
453. https://en.wikipedia.org/wiki/Timeline_of_antisemitism_in_the_20th_century#cite_note-latobit-52
454. https://en.wikipedia.org/wiki/Timeline_of_antisemitism_in_the_20th_century#cite_note-americanexperiencetranscript-53
455. https://en.wikipedia.org/wiki/Timeline_of_antisemitism_in_the_20th_century#cite_note-nymagbess-54

read no coloreds, no Jews, no dogs. I felt so rejected. Here I was chosen to represent American womanhood and then America treated me like this."[54][458] She thus cut short her Miss America tour and instead traveled with the **Anti-Defamation League**[459]. In this capacity, she spoke against discrimination in a talk entitled, "You Can't Be Beautiful and Hate."[52][460][53][461][54][462][55][463][56][464]

1945

The **Kraków pogrom**[465] was a post-WW2 pogrom, resulting in the death of **Auschwitz**[466] survivor **Róża Berger**[467].

---

456. https://en.wikipedia.org/wiki/Timeline_of_antisemitism_in_the_20th_century#cite_note-nytmyobit-55
457. https://en.wikipedia.org/wiki/Timeline_of_antisemitism_in_the_20th_century#cite_note-wsjobitbm-56
458. https://en.wikipedia.org/wiki/Timeline_of_antisemitism_in_the_20th_century#cite_note-nymagbess-54
459. https://en.wikipedia.org/wiki/Anti-Defamation_League
460. https://en.wikipedia.org/wiki/Timeline_of_antisemitism_in_the_20th_century#cite_note-latobit-52
461. https://en.wikipedia.org/wiki/Timeline_of_antisemitism_in_the_20th_century#cite_note-americanexperiencetranscript-53
462. https://en.wikipedia.org/wiki/Timeline_of_antisemitism_in_the_20th_century#cite_note-nymagbess-54
463. https://en.wikipedia.org/wiki/Timeline_of_antisemitism_in_the_20th_century#cite_note-nytmyobit-55
464. https://en.wikipedia.org/wiki/Timeline_of_antisemitism_in_the_20th_century#cite_note-wsjobitbm-56

1946

The **Kielce pogrom**[468]. 40 Jews were massacred and 80 other Jews were wounded out of about 200 who had returned home after **World War II**[469] had ended. 2 non-Jewish Poles were also killed. Controversy was caused by **August Hlond**[470]'s reaction to the **Kielce pogrom**[471]. While condemning murders, Hlond denied the racist nature of this crime.[57][472][58][473] He saw the pogrom as a reaction against Jewish bureaucrats serving the Communist regime.[58][474] This position was echoed by **Cardinal Sapieha**[475], who was reported to have said that the Jews brought it on themselves.[57][476]

1946

465. https://en.wikipedia.org/wiki/Krak%C3%B3w_pogrom
466. https://en.wikipedia.org/wiki/Auschwitz
467. https://en.wikipedia.org/wiki/R%C3%B3%C5%BCa_Berger
468. https://en.wikipedia.org/wiki/Kielce_pogrom
469. https://en.wikipedia.org/wiki/World_War_II
470. https://en.wikipedia.org/wiki/August_Hlond
471. https://en.wikipedia.org/wiki/Kielce_pogrom
472. https://en.wikipedia.org/wiki/Timeline_of_antisemitism_in_the_20th_century#cite_note-Kent-57
473. https://en.wikipedia.org/wiki/Timeline_of_antisemitism_in_the_20th_century#cite_note-Phayer-58
474. https://en.wikipedia.org/wiki/Timeline_of_antisemitism_in_the_20th_century#cite_note-Phayer-58
475. https://en.wikipedia.org/wiki/Cardinal_Sapieha
476. https://en.wikipedia.org/wiki/Timeline_of_antisemitism_in_the_20th_century#cite_note-Kent-57

Nikita Khrushchev[477], then the first secretary of the **Communist party**[478] of **Ukraine**[479], closes many synagogues (the number declines from 450 to 60) and prevents Jewish refugees from returning to their homes.[59][480]

1946

The post-WW2 **Kunmadaras pogrom**[481] was the killing of 6 Jewish **Holocaust**[482] survivors in **Kunmadaras**[483], Hungary.

1946

The **Miskolc pogrom**[484]

1947

Anti-Jewish riots erupt in Aleppo[485], resulting in some 75 Jews murdered and several hundred wounded.

1947

A mob of Muslim sailors looted Jewish homes and shops in the **Manama riots**[486]. In the end one Jewish woman was dead and a Synagogue was destroyed.

1947

---

477. https://en.wikipedia.org/wiki/Nikita_Khrushchev
478. https://en.wikipedia.org/wiki/Communist_party
479. https://en.wikipedia.org/wiki/Ukraine
480. https://en.wikipedia.org/wiki/Timeline_of_antisemitism_in_the_20th_century#cite_note-59
481. https://en.wikipedia.org/wiki/Kunmadaras_pogrom
482. https://en.wikipedia.org/wiki/Holocaust
483. https://en.wikipedia.org/wiki/Kunmadaras
484. https://en.wikipedia.org/wiki/Miskolc_pogrom
485. https://en.wikipedia.org/wiki/1947_anti-Jewish_riots_in_Aleppo
486. https://en.wikipedia.org/wiki/1947_Manama_riots

A three-day riot[487] broke out between the **Jews of Aden**[488] and the local Muslim population. When it was over, 82 Jews were killed and 76 Jews were injured.

1947

In Austria, the **Verbotsgesetz 1947**[489] provided the legal framework for the process of **denazification**[490] in Austria and the suppression of any potential **revival of Nazism**[491]. In 1992, it was amended to prohibit the denial or gross minimisation of the Holocaust.

National Socialism Prohibition Law (1947, amendments of 1992)

§ 3g. He who operates in a manner characterized other than that in § § 3a – 3f will be punished (revitalising of the NSDAP or identification with), with imprisonment from one to up to ten years, and in cases of particularly dangerous suspects or activity, be punished with up to twenty years' imprisonment.[60][492]

§ 3h. As an amendment to § 3 g., whoever denies, grossly plays down, approves or tries to excuse the National Socialist genocide or other National Socialist crimes against humanity in a print publication, in broadcast or other media.[61][493]

1947

The **Aden riots**[494] of December 2–4, 1947 targeted the **Jewish community**[495] in the **British**[496] **Colony of Aden**[497]. At least 76 Jews

---

487. **https://en.wikipedia.org/wiki/1947_Aden_riots**

488. **https://en.wikipedia.org/wiki/Jews_of_Aden**

489. **https://en.wikipedia.org/wiki/Verbotsgesetz_1947**

490. **https://en.wikipedia.org/wiki/Denazification**

491. **https://en.wikipedia.org/wiki/Neo-Nazism**

492. **https://en.wikipedia.org/wiki/Timeline_of_antisemitism_in_the_20th_century#cite_note-austria47-60**

493. **https://en.wikipedia.org/wiki/Timeline_of_antisemitism_in_the_20th_century#cite_note-austria92-61**

were killed. Shortly after the riots, Aden's Jewish community almost entirely left, together with most of the Yemeni Jewish community.

1947

1947 Manama riots[498].

1948–2001

Antisemitism played a central role in the **Jewish exodus from Arab lands**[499]. The Jewish population in the Arab Middle East and North Africa has decreased from 900,000 in 1948 to less than 8,000 in 2001.

1948

The **Djereda**[500] was a pogrom against the tiny Jewish population of **Jerada**[501] at the hands of the local Muslims. It ended with 43 Jews dead and around 150 Jews injured.

1948

The **1948 Anti-Jewish riots in Tripolitania**[502] was a riot between the Jewish and Arab populations of Tripoli. Unlike the **previous Tripoli pogrom**[503], the Jewish community of Tripoli fought back against the Muslim rioters. When it was over, 14 Jews and 4 Muslims were dead and many on both sides were injured.

1948

494. https://en.wikipedia.org/wiki/1947_anti-Jewish_riots_in_Aden
495. https://en.wikipedia.org/wiki/Adeni_Jews
496. https://en.wikipedia.org/wiki/British_Empire
497. https://en.wikipedia.org/wiki/Aden_Colony
498. https://en.wikipedia.org/wiki/1947_Manama_riots
499. https://en.wikipedia.org/wiki/Jewish_exodus_from_Arab_lands
500. https://en.wikipedia.org/wiki/1948_Anti-Jewish_Riots_in_Oujda_and_Jerada
501. https://en.wikipedia.org/wiki/Jerada
502. https://en.wikipedia.org/wiki/1948_Anti-Jewish_riots_in_Tripolitania
503. https://en.wikipedia.org/wiki/1945_Anti-Jewish_riots_in_Tripolitania

The **1948 Cairo bombings**[504] were several bombings which targeted the **Jewish population of Cairo**[505]. The bombings claimed the lives of 70 Jews and 200 other Jews were wounded.

1948

The **Southern Baptist Convention**[506] passed a resolution stating in part, "RESOLVED, That **communism**[507], **fascism**[508], political ecclesiasticism, and anti-Semitism are utterly contrary to the genius of our Baptist concept of freedom and spiritual values."[62][509]

1948

Solomon Mikhoels[510], actor-director of the **Moscow State Jewish Theater**[511] and chairman of the **Jewish Anti-Fascist Committee**[512] is killed in a suspicious car accident (see **MGB**[513]). Mass arrests of prominent Jewish intellectuals and suppression of Jewish culture follow under the banners of campaign on ***rootless cosmopolitanism***[514] and ***anti-Zionism***[515].

1948

---

504. https://en.wikipedia.org/wiki/1948_Cairo_bombings
505. https://en.wikipedia.org/wiki/Egyptian_Jews
506. https://en.wikipedia.org/wiki/Southern_Baptist_Convention
507. https://en.wikipedia.org/wiki/Communism
508. https://en.wikipedia.org/wiki/Fascism
509. https://en.wikipedia.org/wiki/Timeline_of_antisemitism_in_the_20th_century#cite_note-62
510. https://en.wikipedia.org/wiki/Solomon_Mikhoels
511. https://en.wikipedia.org/wiki/Moscow_State_Jewish_Theater
512. https://en.wikipedia.org/wiki/Jewish_Anti-Fascist_Committee
513. https://en.wikipedia.org/wiki/MGB_(USSR)
514. *https://en.wikipedia.org/wiki/Rootless_cosmopolitan*
515. *https://en.wikipedia.org/wiki/Anti-Zionism*

During the **Siege of Jerusalem**[516] of the **1948 Arab–Israeli War**[517], Arab armies were able to conquer the part of the West Bank and Jerusalem; they expelled all Jews (about 2,000) from the **Old City**[518] (the **Jewish Quarter**[519]) and destroyed the ancient synagogues that were in the Old City as well.

1949

The **Menarsha synagogue attack**[520] was a grenade attack in the Jewish quarter of **Damascus**[521] that took 12 lives.

1950s[edit[522]]

1952

The **Night of the Murdered Poets**[523]. The thirteen most prominent Soviet Yiddish writers, poets, actors and other intellectuals were executed, among them **Peretz Markish**[524], **Leib Kwitko**[525], **David Hofstein**[526], **Itzik Feffer**[527], **David Bergelson**[528].[63]529[64]530 In

516. https://en.wikipedia.org/wiki/Battle_for_Jerusalem_(1948)
517. https://en.wikipedia.org/wiki/1948_Arab%E2%80%93Israeli_War
518. https://en.wikipedia.org/wiki/Old_City_(Jerusalem)
519. https://en.wikipedia.org/wiki/Jewish_Quarter_(Jerusalem)
520. https://en.wikipedia.org/wiki/Menarsha_synagogue_attack
521. https://en.wikipedia.org/wiki/Damascus
522. https://en.wikipedia.org/w/index.php?title=Timeline_of_antisemitism_in_the_20th_century&action=edit§ion=6
523. https://en.wikipedia.org/wiki/Night_of_the_Murdered_Poets
524. https://en.wikipedia.org/wiki/Peretz_Markish
525. https://en.wikipedia.org/wiki/Leib_Kwitko
526. https://en.wikipedia.org/wiki/David_Hofstein
527. https://en.wikipedia.org/wiki/Itzik_Feffer

1955 UN General Assembly's session a high Soviet official still denied the "rumors" about their disappearance.

1952

The **Prague Trials**[531] in **Czechoslovakia**[532].

1953

The **Doctors' plot**[533] false accusation in the **USSR**[534]. Scores of Soviet Jews dismissed from their jobs, arrested, some executed. The USSR was accused of pursuing a "new antisemitism."[65][535] Stalinist opposition to "**rootless cosmopolitans**[536]" – a euphemism for Jews – was rooted in the belief, as expressed by **Klement Gottwald**[537], that "treason and espionage infiltrate the ranks of the Communist Party. This channel is **Zionism**[538]."[66][539] This newer antisemitism was, in effect, a species of anti-Zionism.

1953

528. https://en.wikipedia.org/wiki/David_Bergelson
529. https://en.wikipedia.org/wiki/Timeline_of_antisemitism_in_the_20th_century#cite_note-63
530. https://en.wikipedia.org/wiki/Timeline_of_antisemitism_in_the_20th_century#cite_note-64
531. https://en.wikipedia.org/wiki/Prague_Trials
532. https://en.wikipedia.org/wiki/Czechoslovakia
533. https://en.wikipedia.org/wiki/Doctors%27_plot
534. https://en.wikipedia.org/wiki/Soviet_Union
535. https://en.wikipedia.org/wiki/Timeline_of_antisemitism_in_the_20th_century#cite_note-65
536. https://en.wikipedia.org/wiki/Rootless_cosmopolitan
537. https://en.wikipedia.org/wiki/Klement_Gottwald
538. https://en.wikipedia.org/wiki/Zionism

Holocaust Remembrance Day in Israel is inaugurated.[67][540]

1956

The **Alaska Mental Health Enabling Act**[541] of 1956 (**Public Law**[542] 84-830) was an **Act of Congress**[543] passed to improve **mental health**[544] care in the United States **territory**[545] of **Alaska**[546]. It became the focus of a major political controversy[68][547] after opponents nicknamed it the "**Siberia**[548] Bill" and denounced it as being part of a **communist**[549] plot to hospitalize and **brainwash**[550] Americans. Campaigners asserted that it was part of an international Jewish,

---

539. https://en.wikipedia.org/wiki/Timeline_of_antisemitism_in_the_20th_century#cite_note-66
540. https://en.wikipedia.org/wiki/Timeline_of_antisemitism_in_the_20th_century#cite_note-calendar-67
541. https://en.wikipedia.org/wiki/Alaska_Mental_Health_Enabling_Act
542. https://en.wikipedia.org/wiki/Act_of_Congress
543. https://en.wikipedia.org/wiki/Act_of_Congress
544. https://en.wikipedia.org/wiki/Mental_health
545. https://en.wikipedia.org/wiki/Alaska_Territory
546. https://en.wikipedia.org/wiki/Alaska
547. https://en.wikipedia.org/wiki/Timeline_of_antisemitism_in_the_20th_century#cite_note-68
548. https://en.wikipedia.org/wiki/Siberia
549. https://en.wikipedia.org/wiki/Communism
550. https://en.wikipedia.org/wiki/Brainwashing

Roman Catholic[551] or **psychiatric**[552] conspiracy intended to establish United Nations-run **concentration camps**[553] in the United States.

1956

Antisemitism swept across Poland as part of a purge of Stalinists.[69][554]

1958

On 28 April 1958, Birmingham, Alabama, 54 sticks of **dynamite**[555] were placed outside **Temple Beth-El**[556] in a bombing attempt. According to police reports, the burning fuses were doused by heavy rainfall, preventing the dynamite from exploding.[70][557] Although the crime was never solved, police considered **Bobby Frank Cherry**[558], later convicted of bombing the **Sixteenth Street Baptist Church**[559], to be a suspect.[71][560]

1958

---

551. https://en.wikipedia.org/wiki/Roman_Catholic_Church
552. https://en.wikipedia.org/wiki/Psychiatry
553. https://en.wikipedia.org/wiki/Concentration_camp
554. https://en.wikipedia.org/wiki/Timeline_of_antisemitism_in_the_20th_century#cite_note-jweekly1968-69
555. https://en.wikipedia.org/wiki/Dynamite
556. https://en.wikipedia.org/wiki/Temple_Beth-El_(Birmingham,_Alabama)
557. https://en.wikipedia.org/wiki/Timeline_of_antisemitism_in_the_20th_century#cite_note-70
558. https://en.wikipedia.org/wiki/Bobby_Frank_Cherry
559. https://en.wikipedia.org/wiki/16th_Street_Baptist_Church_bombing
560. https://en.wikipedia.org/wiki/Timeline_of_antisemitism_in_the_20th_century#cite_note-71

The **Hebrew Benevolent Congregation Temple bombing**[561] occurred on 12 October 1958. The **Temple**[562], on **Peachtree Street**[563] in **Atlanta**[564], Georgia, housed a **Reform Jewish**[565] congregation. The building was damaged extensively by the dynamite-fueled explosion, although no one was injured. Five suspects were arrested almost immediately after the bombing. One of them, George Bright, was tried twice. His first trial ended with a hung jury and his second with an acquittal. As a result of Bright's acquittal the other suspects were not tried, and no one was ever convicted of the bombing.

1959

Impeachment of Man[566] is a book by **Savitri Devi**[567], first published in 1959, in which she recounts a history of the general indifference toward the suffering of non-human life. She puts forth a pro-vegetarian, anti-**vivisectionist**[568], **biocentric**[569], and **misanthropic**[570] **conservationist**[571] point of view. However, she does so within the context of her pro-**Hitler**[572] and pro-**Nazi**[573] political views, and devotes space to antisemitism and denouncing Jewish dietary practices.

---

561. https://en.wikipedia.org/wiki/Hebrew_Benevolent_Congregation_Temple_bombing
562. https://en.wikipedia.org/wiki/The_Temple_(Atlanta)
563. https://en.wikipedia.org/wiki/Peachtree_Street
564. https://en.wikipedia.org/wiki/Atlanta
565. https://en.wikipedia.org/wiki/Reform_Judaism
566. *https://en.wikipedia.org/wiki/Impeachment_of_Man*
567. https://en.wikipedia.org/wiki/Savitri_Devi
568. https://en.wikipedia.org/wiki/Vivisection
569. https://en.wikipedia.org/wiki/Biocentrism_(ethics)
570. https://en.wikipedia.org/wiki/Misanthropic
571. https://en.wikipedia.org/wiki/Conservation_movement
572. https://en.wikipedia.org/wiki/Hitler
573. https://en.wikipedia.org/wiki/Nazism

1959

On 21 March 1959, **Pope John XXIII**[574] ordered that the word "faithless" (**Latin**[575]: *perfidis*) be removed from the prayer for the conversion of the Jews,[72][576] actually interrupting the Service and asking the prayer to be repeated without that word.[73][577]: 40 This word had caused much trouble in recent times because of misconceptions that the **Latin**[578] *perfidis* was equivalent to "**perfidious**[579]", giving birth to the view that the prayer accused the Jews of treachery (perfidy), though the word is more correctly translated as "faithless" or "unbelieving".[74][580] Accordingly, the prayer was revised to read:

Let us pray also for the Jews: that almighty God may remove the veil from their hearts; so that they too may acknowledge Jesus Christ our Lord. Let us pray. Let us kneel. Arise. Almighty and eternal God, who dost also not exclude from thy mercy the Jews: hear our prayers, which we offer for the blindness of that people; that acknowledging

---

574. **https://en.wikipedia.org/wiki/Pope_John_XXIII**
575. **https://en.wikipedia.org/wiki/Latin_language**
576. **https://en.wikipedia.org/wiki/Timeline_of_antisemitism_in_the_20th_century#cite_note-72**
577. **https://en.wikipedia.org/wiki/Timeline_of_antisemitism_in_the_20th_century#cite_note-73**
578. **https://en.wikipedia.org/wiki/Latin**
579. **https://en.wiktionary.org/wiki/perfidious**
580. **https://en.wikipedia.org/wiki/Timeline_of_antisemitism_in_the_20th_century#cite_note-74**

the light of thy Truth, which is Christ, they may be delivered from their darkness. Through the same our Lord Jesus Christ, who liveth and reigneth with thee in the unity of the Holy Spirit, God, for ever and ever. Amen.[75][581] On Good Friday of 1963,[76][582] by mistake the old text of the prayer was given to the deacon, who read "perfidis". **Pope John XXIII**[583] interrupted the liturgy again, and ordered that the prayer be repeated with the word omitted.[77][584]

1960s[edit[585]]

1960s

Chess player **Bobby Fischer**[586] made numerous anti-Jewish statements and professed a general hatred for Jews since at least the early 1960s.[78][587][79][588] Although Fischer described his mother as Jewish in a 1962 interview,[78][589] he later denied his Jewish ancestry.[80][590]

---

581. https://en.wikipedia.org/wiki/Timeline_of_antisemitism_in_the_20th_century#cite_note-75
582. https://en.wikipedia.org/wiki/Timeline_of_antisemitism_in_the_20th_century#cite_note-zenit-76
583. https://en.wikipedia.org/wiki/Pope_John_XXIII
584. https://en.wikipedia.org/wiki/Timeline_of_antisemitism_in_the_20th_century#cite_note-77
585. https://en.wikipedia.org/w/index.php?title=Timeline_of_antisemitism_in_the_20th_century&action=edit§ion=7
586. https://en.wikipedia.org/wiki/Bobby_Fischer

1960

The Badges Act 1960 (Abzeichengesetz 1960) prohibits the public display of Nazi symbols in Austria, and violations are punishable by up to €4000.- fine and up to 1 month imprisonment.

1960

On 25 March,[81][591] 1960, the synagogue **Congregation Beth Israel**[592] and its members were subject to an **antisemitic**[593] attack. About 180 members were attending a Friday evening service to dedicate the new Zemurray Social Hall, and led by then-rabbi Saul Rubin and Rev. John Speaks and Dr. Franklin Denson of First Methodist Church, when windows were smashed and the synagogue **fire-bombed**[594]. Two members—Alvin Lowi and Alan Cohn—who

587. https://en.wikipedia.org/wiki/Timeline_of_antisemitism_in_the_20th_century#cite_note-Fischer-Harper-78

588. https://en.wikipedia.org/wiki/Timeline_of_antisemitism_in_the_20th_century#cite_note-79

589. https://en.wikipedia.org/wiki/Timeline_of_antisemitism_in_the_20th_century#cite_note-Fischer-Harper-78

590. https://en.wikipedia.org/wiki/Timeline_of_antisemitism_in_the_20th_century#cite_note-la-times-80

591. https://en.wikipedia.org/wiki/Timeline_of_antisemitism_in_the_20th_century#cite_note-DateOfAttack-81

592. https://en.wikipedia.org/wiki/Congregation_Beth_Israel_(Gadsden,_Alabama)

593. https://en.wikipedia.org/wiki/Antisemitism

594. https://en.wikipedia.org/wiki/Firebombing

rushed out to see what was happening were met by Jerry Hunt, a 16-year-old **Nazi sympathizer**[595], who wounded them both with a shotgun, then fled. Lowi was just shot in the hand, but one of Cohn's aortas was nicked, and he almost died, requiring 22 US pints (10 L) of blood.[82][596][83][597][84][598] Earlier that week Hunt had attended a rally for antisemitic and **white supremacist**[599] politician **John G. Crommelin**[600], and had had a fight with a Jewish boy over a chess game at the Gadsden Community Centre.[82][601]

1961

In 1961, a protégé of **Harry Elmer Barnes**[602], **David Hoggan**[603] published *Der Erzwungene Krieg* (*The Forced War*) in West Germany, which claimed that Germany had been the victim of an Anglo-Polish

595. https://en.wikipedia.org/wiki/Neo-Nazism

596. https://en.wikipedia.org/wiki/Timeline_of_antisemitism_in_the_20th_century#cite_note-ISJL-82

597. https://en.wikipedia.org/wiki/Timeline_of_antisemitism_in_the_20th_century#cite_note-Webb2003pp142-143-83

598. https://en.wikipedia.org/wiki/Timeline_of_antisemitism_in_the_20th_century#cite_note-AHAv25i1p13-84

599. https://en.wikipedia.org/wiki/White_supremacism

600. https://en.wikipedia.org/wiki/John_G._Crommelin

601. https://en.wikipedia.org/wiki/Timeline_of_antisemitism_in_the_20th_century#cite_note-ISJL-82

602. https://en.wikipedia.org/wiki/Harry_Elmer_Barnes

603. https://en.wikipedia.org/wiki/David_Hoggan

conspiracy in 1939. Though *Der Erzwungene Krieg* was primarily concerned with the origins of World War II, it also down-played or justified the effects of Nazi **antisemitic**[604] measures in the pre-1939 period.[85][605] For example, Hoggan justified the huge one billion *Reich*-mark fine imposed on the entire Jewish community in Germany after the 1938 ***Kristallnacht***[606] as a reasonable measure to prevent what he called "Jewish profiteering" at the expense of German insurance companies and alleged that no Jews were killed in the *Kristallnacht* (in fact, 91 German Jews were killed in the *Kristallnacht*).[85][607]

1962

In his 1962 pamphlet, *Revisionism and Brainwashing*, **Harry Elmer Barnes**[608] claimed that there was a "lack of any serious opposition or concerted challenge to the atrocity stories and other modes of defamation of German national character and conduct".[86][609] Barnes argued that there was "a failure to point out the

---

604. https://en.wikipedia.org/wiki/Antisemitic

605. https://en.wikipedia.org/wiki/Timeline_of_antisemitism_in_the_20th_century#cite_note-Lipstadt_c0cb5f0fcf239ab3d9c1fcd31fff1efc__Deborah_page_71-85

606. https://en.wikipedia.org/wiki/Kristallnacht

607. https://en.wikipedia.org/wiki/Timeline_of_antisemitism_in_the_20th_century#cite_note-Lipstadt_c0cb5f0fcf239ab3d9c1fcd31fff1efc__Deborah_page_71-85

608. https://en.wikipedia.org/wiki/Harry_Elmer_Barnes

609. https://en.wikipedia.org/wiki/Timeline_of_antisemitism_in_the_20th_century#cite_note-86

atrocities of the Allies were more brutal, painful, mortal and numerous than the most extreme allegations made against the Germans".[87][610] He claimed that in order to justify the "horrors and evils of the Second World War", the Allies made the Nazis the "scapegoat" for their own misdeeds.[88][611]

1963

"Judaism Without Embellishments" published by the Academy of Sciences of the Ukrainian SSR in 1963.

1964

In a 1964 article, "Zionist Fraud", published in the ***American Mercury***[612], **Harry Elmer Barnes**[613] wrote: "The courageous author [Rassinier] lays the chief blame for misrepresentation on those whom we must call the swindlers of the crematoria, the Israeli politicians who derive billions of marks from nonexistent, mythical and imaginary cadavers, whose numbers have been reckoned in an unusually distorted and dishonest manner."[89][614] Using Rassinier as his source, Barnes claimed that Germany was the victim of aggression in both 1914 and

---

610. https://en.wikipedia.org/wiki/Timeline_of_antisemitism_in_the_20th_century#cite_note-Lipstadt_c0cb5f0fcf239ab3d9c1fcd31fff1efc__Deborah_page_74-87

611. https://en.wikipedia.org/wiki/Timeline_of_antisemitism_in_the_20th_century#cite_note-88

612. *https://en.wikipedia.org/wiki/American_Mercury*

613. https://en.wikipedia.org/wiki/Harry_Elmer_Barnes

614. https://en.wikipedia.org/wiki/Timeline_of_antisemitism_in_the_20th_century#cite_note-89

1939, and that reports of the Holocaust were propaganda to justify a war of aggression against Germany.[87][615]

1964

Nasser[616] told a German newspaper in 1964 that "no person, not even the most simple one, takes seriously the lie of the six million Jews that were murdered [in the Holocaust]."[90][617][91][618]

1964

The **Roman Catholic Church**[619] under **Pope Paul VI**[620] issues the document ***Nostra aetate***[621] as part of **Vatican II**[622], repudiating the doctrine of **Jewish guilt**[623] for the **Crucifixion**[624].

1964

In 1964, French historian **Paul Rassinier**[625] published *The Drama of the European Jews.* Rassinier was himself a concentration camp

---

615. https://en.wikipedia.org/wiki/Timeline_of_antisemitism_in_the_20th_century#cite_note-Lipstadt_c0cb5f0fcf239ab3d9c1fcd31fff1efc__Deborah_page_74-87
616. https://en.wikipedia.org/wiki/Gamal_Abdel_Nasser
617. https://en.wikipedia.org/wiki/Timeline_of_antisemitism_in_the_20th_century#cite_note-90
618. https://en.wikipedia.org/wiki/Timeline_of_antisemitism_in_the_20th_century#cite_note-91
619. https://en.wikipedia.org/wiki/Roman_Catholic_Church
620. https://en.wikipedia.org/wiki/Pope_Paul_VI
621. *https://en.wikipedia.org/wiki/Nostra_aetate*
622. https://en.wikipedia.org/wiki/Vatican_II
623. https://en.wikipedia.org/w/index.php?title=Jewish_guilt&action=edit&redlink=1
624. https://en.wikipedia.org/wiki/Crucifixion
625. https://en.wikipedia.org/wiki/Paul_Rassinier

survivor (he was held in **Buchenwald**[626] for having helped French Jews escape the Nazis), and modern-day holocaust deniers continue to cite his works as scholarly research that questions the accepted facts of the Holocaust. Critics argued that Rassinier did not cite evidence for his claims and ignored information that contradicted his assertions; he nevertheless remains influential in Holocaust denial circles for being one of the first deniers to propose that a vast Zionist/Allied/Soviet conspiracy faked the Holocaust, a theme that would be picked up in later years by other authors.[92][627]

1964

The **Civil Rights Act of 1964**[628] (**Pub. L.**[629]Tooltip Public Law (United States) **88–352**[630], 78 **Stat.**[631] **241**[632], enacted July 2, 1964) is a landmark piece of **civil rights**[633] legislation in the United States[93][634] that outlawed discrimination based on religion, race, color, sex, or national origin.[94][635]

1965

---

626. https://en.wikipedia.org/wiki/Buchenwald

627. https://en.wikipedia.org/wiki/Timeline_of_antisemitism_in_the_20th_century#cite_note-92

628. https://en.wikipedia.org/wiki/Civil_Rights_Act_of_1964

629. https://en.wikipedia.org/wiki/Public_Law_(United_States)

630. https://uslaw.link/citation/us-law/public/88/352

631. https://en.wikipedia.org/wiki/United_States_Statutes_at_Large

632. https://legislink.org/us/stat-78-241

633. https://en.wikipedia.org/wiki/Civil_rights

634. https://en.wikipedia.org/wiki/Timeline_of_antisemitism_in_the_20th_century#cite_note-93

The **Frankfurt Auschwitz trials**[636], known in German as *der Auschwitz-Prozess*, or *der zweite Auschwitz-Prozess,* (the "second Auschwitz trial") was a series of trials running from 20 December 1963 to 19 August 1965, charging 22 defendants under German **criminal law**[637] for their roles in the **Holocaust**[638] as mid- to lower-level officials in the **Auschwitz-Birkenau**[639] **death**[640] and **concentration camp**[641] complex. **Hans Hofmeyer**[642] led as Chief Judge the "criminal case against **Mulka**[643] and others" (reference number 4 Ks 2/63).

Overall, only 789 individuals of the approximately 6,500 surviving *SS* personnel who served at Auschwitz and its sub-camps were ever tried, of which 750 received sentences.[95][644] Unlike the first trial in Poland held almost two decades earlier, the trials in Frankfurt were not based on the legal definition of **crimes against humanity**[645] as recognized by international law, but according to the state laws of the Federal Republic.[96][646]

1967

---

635. **https://en.wikipedia.org/wiki/Timeline_of_antisemitism_in_the_20th_century#cite_note-94**

636. **https://en.wikipedia.org/wiki/Frankfurt_Auschwitz_trials**

637. **https://en.wikipedia.org/wiki/Criminal_law**

638. **https://en.wikipedia.org/wiki/Holocaust**

639. **https://en.wikipedia.org/wiki/Auschwitz-Birkenau**

640. **https://en.wikipedia.org/wiki/Death_camp**

641. **https://en.wikipedia.org/wiki/Concentration_camp**

642. **https://en.wikipedia.org/wiki/Hans_Hofmeyer**

643. **https://en.wikipedia.org/wiki/Robert_Mulka**

644. **https://en.wikipedia.org/wiki/Timeline_of_antisemitism_in_the_20th_century#cite_note-95**

645. **https://en.wikipedia.org/wiki/Crimes_against_humanity**

Allen Ginsberg[647] stated that, in a private conversation in 1967, **Ezra Pound**[648] told the young poet, "my poems don't make sense." He went on to supposedly call himself a "moron", to characterize his writing as "stupid and ignorant", "a mess". Ginsberg reassured Pound that he "had shown us the way", but Pound refused to be mollified:

'Any good I've done has been spoiled by bad intentions – the preoccupation with irrelevant and stupid things,' [he] replied. Then very slowly, with emphasis, surely conscious of Ginsberg's being Jewish: 'But the worst mistake I made was that stupid, suburban prejudice of anti-semitism.'[97][649]

1967

In 1967, **Congregation Beth Israel**[650] moved to its current location, a building on Old Canton Road[98][651] described by **Jack Nelson**[652] as "an octagonal structure dominated by a massive roof".[99][653] On 18 September 1967 the new building was wrecked by a dynamite bomb placed by Klan members in a recessed

646. https://en.wikipedia.org/wiki/Timeline_of_antisemitism_in_the_20th_century#cite_note-Shik-2014-96

647. https://en.wikipedia.org/wiki/Allen_Ginsberg

648. https://en.wikipedia.org/wiki/Ezra_Pound

649. https://en.wikipedia.org/wiki/Timeline_of_antisemitism_in_the_20th_century#cite_note-Carpenter898ff-97

650. https://en.wikipedia.org/wiki/Congregation_Beth_Israel_(Jackson,_Mississippi)

651. https://en.wikipedia.org/wiki/Timeline_of_antisemitism_in_the_20th_century#cite_note-history-98

652. https://en.wikipedia.org/wiki/Jack_Nelson_(journalist)

653. https://en.wikipedia.org/wiki/Timeline_of_antisemitism_in_the_20th_century#cite_note-99

doorway.[100][654][101][655][102][656] According to Nelson, the explosion had "ripped through administrative offices and a conference room, torn a hole in the ceiling, blown out windows, ruptured a water pipe and buckled a wall."[103][657] The perpetrators were not discovered.[101][658] In November of that year the same group planted a bomb that blew out the front of the house of Dr. Perry Nussbaum (Beth Israel's rabbi from 1954 to 1973), while he and his wife were sleeping there.[100][659][101][660][102][661]

1967

---

654. https://en.wikipedia.org/wiki/Timeline_of_antisemitism_in_the_20th_century#cite_note-ISJLBIJackson-100
655. https://en.wikipedia.org/wiki/Timeline_of_antisemitism_in_the_20th_century#cite_note-Sparks2001p239-101
656. https://en.wikipedia.org/wiki/Timeline_of_antisemitism_in_the_20th_century#cite_note-Chalmers2003p82-102
657. https://en.wikipedia.org/wiki/Timeline_of_antisemitism_in_the_20th_century#cite_note-Nelson1993p32-103
658. https://en.wikipedia.org/wiki/Timeline_of_antisemitism_in_the_20th_century#cite_note-Sparks2001p239-101
659. https://en.wikipedia.org/wiki/Timeline_of_antisemitism_in_the_20th_century#cite_note-ISJLBIJackson-100

All Jewish men in Egypt were placed in camps in 1967 during the **Six-Day War**[662], and they were kept there for more than two years; **Karaite Jews**[663] were the last to leave.[104][664]

1968–1971

State-supported anti-Semitism swept across Poland in 1968, not subsiding until 1971, by which time half of Poland's Jews had fled Poland.[69][665]

1968

During the **American Civil Rights Movement**[666] in the 1960s, the leadership of **Beth Israel**[667] spoke out against the **Ku Klux Klan**[668]'s attacks on black churches. In response, Thomas Tarrants of **Mobile, Alabama**[669], who had helped bomb the synagogue building

---

660. https://en.wikipedia.org/wiki/Timeline_of_antisemitism_in_the_20th_century#cite_note-Sparks2001p239-101
661. https://en.wikipedia.org/wiki/Timeline_of_antisemitism_in_the_20th_century#cite_note-Chalmers2003p82-102
662. https://en.wikipedia.org/wiki/Six-Day_War
663. https://en.wikipedia.org/wiki/Karaite_Judaism
664. https://en.wikipedia.org/wiki/Timeline_of_antisemitism_in_the_20th_century#cite_note-104
665. https://en.wikipedia.org/wiki/Timeline_of_antisemitism_in_the_20th_century#cite_note-jweekly1968-69
666. https://en.wikipedia.org/wiki/American_Civil_Rights_Movement
667. https://en.wikipedia.org/wiki/Congregation_Beth_Israel_(Jackson,_Mississippi)
668. https://en.wikipedia.org/wiki/Ku_Klux_Klan

of a different synagogue, **Beth Israel Congregation**[670], and its rabbi's house there (see previous entry in this timeline)[105][671][106][672] bombed Beth Israel's education building on 28 May 1968.[107][673][108][674] The force of the blast knocked down several walls of the education building and caved in part of the roof while also destroying a door at the opposite end of the synagogue building.[108][675] A hole approximately 24 inches (61 cm) in diameter was left in the concrete floor, and damages were estimated to be around $50,000 (equivalent to $438,000 today).[109][676] According to Sammy Feltenstein, past president of Congregation Beth Israel, pieces of stained glass that survived the bombing were salvaged and adorn the

---

669. https://en.wikipedia.org/wiki/Mobile,_Alabama
670. https://en.wikipedia.org/wiki/Beth_Israel_Congregation_(Jackson,_Mississippi)
671. https://en.wikipedia.org/wiki/Timeline_of_antisemitism_in_the_20th_century#cite_note-meridianjews-105
672. https://en.wikipedia.org/wiki/Timeline_of_antisemitism_in_the_20th_century#cite_note-terror-106
673. https://en.wikipedia.org/wiki/Timeline_of_antisemitism_in_the_20th_century#cite_note-bethhistory-107
674. https://en.wikipedia.org/wiki/Timeline_of_antisemitism_in_the_20th_century#cite_note-rome-108
675. https://en.wikipedia.org/wiki/Timeline_of_antisemitism_in_the_20th_century#cite_note-rome-108
676. https://en.wikipedia.org/wiki/Timeline_of_antisemitism_in_the_20th_century#cite_note-timesdaily-109

front window of the synagogue today.[110][677] Later that year, on 30 June, Tarrants[111][678] returned to Meridian to bomb the home of Meyer Davidson, an outspoken leader of the Jewish community, on 29th Avenue.[107][679][110][680] But the **FBI**[681] and police chief Roy Gunn convinced Raymond and Alton Wayne Roberts, local Klan members, to gather information about the Klan's operations, and leaders of the Jewish communities in Jackson and in Meridian had raised money to pay the two informants, who tipped off the FBI about the attack before it happened.[105][682]

1969

David Hoggan[683] explicitly denied the Holocaust in 1969 in a book entitled *The Myth of the Six Million*, which was published by

---

677. https://en.wikipedia.org/wiki/Timeline_of_antisemitism_in_the_20th_century#cite_note-influence-110

678. https://en.wikipedia.org/wiki/Timeline_of_antisemitism_in_the_20th_century#cite_note-tuscaloosa-111

679. https://en.wikipedia.org/wiki/Timeline_of_antisemitism_in_the_20th_century#cite_note-bethhistory-107

680. https://en.wikipedia.org/wiki/Timeline_of_antisemitism_in_the_20th_century#cite_note-influence-110

681. https://en.wikipedia.org/wiki/FBI

682. https://en.wikipedia.org/wiki/Timeline_of_antisemitism_in_the_20th_century#cite_note-meridianjews-105

683. https://en.wikipedia.org/wiki/David_Hoggan

the **Noontide Press**[684], a small Los Angeles publisher specializing in antisemitic literature.[112][685]

1960s–1991

The rise of ***Zionology***[686] in the **Soviet Union**[687]. In 1983, the Department of Propaganda and the **KGB**[688]'s **Anti-Zionist committee of the Soviet public**[689] orchestrates formally "anti-Zionist" campaign.

1968

Polish 1968 political crisis[690]. The state-organized antisemitic campaign in the **People's Republic of Poland**[691] under guise of "anti-Zionism" drives out most of remaining Jewish population.

1968

The ancient Jewish community of **Hebron**[692], which had been destroyed in the **1929 Hebron massacre**[693], is revived at **Kiryat Arba**[694]. The community, in 1979 and afterwards, moves into Hebron proper and rebuilds the demolished **Abraham Avinu Synagogue**[695], the site of which had been used by **Jordan**[696] as a cattle-pen.

---

684. https://en.wikipedia.org/wiki/Noontide_Press

685. https://en.wikipedia.org/wiki/Timeline_of_antisemitism_in_the_20th_century#cite_note-112

686. *https://en.wikipedia.org/wiki/Zionology*

687. https://en.wikipedia.org/wiki/Soviet_Union

688. https://en.wikipedia.org/wiki/KGB

689. https://en.wikipedia.org/wiki/Anti-Zionist_committee_of_the_Soviet_public

690. https://en.wikipedia.org/wiki/1968_Polish_political_crisis

691. https://en.wikipedia.org/wiki/People%27s_Republic_of_Poland

692. https://en.wikipedia.org/wiki/Hebron

693. https://en.wikipedia.org/wiki/1929_Hebron_massacre

694. https://en.wikipedia.org/wiki/Kiryat_Arba

695. https://en.wikipedia.org/wiki/Avraham_Avinu_Synagogue

696. https://en.wikipedia.org/wiki/Jordan

1968

The **Alhambra Decree**[697] was formally revoked on 16 December 1968.[113][698]

1968

The ***Fair Housing Act***[699] (Title VIII of the *Civil Rights Act of 1968*) in the United States introduced meaningful federal enforcement mechanisms. It outlawed:

◈ Refusal to sell or rent a dwelling to any person because of **race**[700], **color**[701], religion, sex, or **national origin**[702].

◈ Discrimination based on race, color, religion or national origin in the terms, conditions or privilege of the sale or rental of a dwelling.

◈ Advertising the sale or rental of a dwelling indicating preference of discrimination based on race, color, religion or national origin.

◈ Coercing, threatening, intimidating, or interfering with a person's enjoyment or exercise of housing rights based on discriminatory reasons or retaliating against a person or organization that aids or encourages the exercise or enjoyment of fair housing rights.

1969 November 9

Tupamaros West-Berlin[703] attempted to bomb of **West Berlin**[704]'s **Jewish Community Centre**[705]. The bomb, supplied by the

---

697. https://en.wikipedia.org/wiki/Alhambra_Decree

698. https://en.wikipedia.org/wiki/Timeline_of_antisemitism_in_the_20th_century#cite_note-nytimes1968-113

699. *https://en.wikipedia.org/wiki/Fair_Housing_Act*

700. https://en.wikipedia.org/wiki/Race_(human_classification)

701. https://en.wikipedia.org/wiki/Human_skin_color

702. https://en.wikipedia.org/wiki/National_origin

703. https://en.wikipedia.org/wiki/Tupamaros_West-Berlin

704. https://en.wikipedia.org/wiki/West_Berlin

undercover government agent **Peter Urbach**[706], failed to explode.[114][707][115][708]

1970s[edit[709]]

1970s

Lyndon LaRouche[710] and his ideas have been called antisemitic since at least the mid-1970s by dozens of individuals and organizations in countries across Europe and North America. LaRouche and his followers have responded to these allegations by claiming that LaRouche has Jewish supporters and by denying the accusations.

1970

Canada has no legislation specifically restricting the ownership, display, purchase, import or export of Nazi flags. However, sections 318–320 of the Criminal Code,[116][711] adopted by **Canada's parliament**[712] in 1970 and based in large part on the 1965 Cohen

705. https://en.wikipedia.org/wiki/Fasanenstrasse_Synagogue#Jewish_Community_Center
706. https://en.wikipedia.org/wiki/Peter_Urbach
707. https://en.wikipedia.org/wiki/Timeline_of_antisemitism_in_the_20th_century#cite_note-sign-114
708. https://en.wikipedia.org/wiki/Timeline_of_antisemitism_in_the_20th_century#cite_note-115
709. https://en.wikipedia.org/w/index.php?title=Timeline_of_antisemitism_in_the_20th_century&action=edit§ion=8
710. https://en.wikipedia.org/wiki/Lyndon_LaRouche
711. https://en.wikipedia.org/wiki/Timeline_of_antisemitism_in_the_20th_century#cite_note-116

Committee recommendations,[117][713] provide law enforcement agencies with broad scope to intervene if such flags are used to communicate hatred in a public place (particularly sections 319(1), 319(2), and 319(7).[117][714]

1970

After the **Second Vatican Council**[715], the **Good Friday prayer for the Jews**[716] was completely revised for the 1970 edition of the Roman Missal. Because of the possibility of a misinterpretation similar to that of the word "perfidis" (see above in 1959), the reference to the veil on the hearts of the Jews, which was based on **2 Corinthians 3:14**[717], was removed. The 1973 **ICEL**[718] English translation of the revised prayer is as follows:

Let us pray for the Jewish people, the first to hear the word of God, that they may continue to grow in the love of his name and in faithfulness to his covenant. (*Prayer in silence. Then the priest says:*) Almighty and eternal God, long ago you gave your promise to Abraham and his posterity. Listen to your Church as we pray that

---

712. https://en.wikipedia.org/wiki/Parliament_of_Canada

713. https://en.wikipedia.org/wiki/Timeline_of_antisemitism_in_the_20th_century#cite_note-HatePropaganda-117

714. https://en.wikipedia.org/wiki/Timeline_of_antisemitism_in_the_20th_century#cite_note-HatePropaganda-117

715. https://en.wikipedia.org/wiki/Second_Vatican_Council

716. https://en.wikipedia.org/wiki/Good_Friday_prayer_for_the_Jews

717. https://bible.oremus.org/?passage=2%20Corinthians%203:14&version=nrsv

718. https://en.wikipedia.org/wiki/ICEL

the people you first made your own may arrive at the fullness of redemption. We ask this through Christ our Lord. Amen.[118][719]

1971

The ban on Jewish immigration to Israel from the Soviet Union was lifted in 1971 leading to the **1970s Soviet Union aliyah**[720].

1971

The **Southern Baptist Convention**[721] passed a resolution stating in part, "we point out particularly one area of concern known as anti-Semitism, which some think erroneously is inherent in Christianity, and which we disavow."[119][722]

1971

To further the goal of reconciliation, the Catholic Church established an internal **International Catholic-Jewish Liaison Committee**[723] and the **International Jewish Committee for Interreligious Consultations**[724]. (This Committee is not a part of the Church's **Magisterium**[725].)

1972

The **Southern Baptist Convention**[726] passed a "Resolution on Anti-Semitism" stating in part:

---

719. https://en.wikipedia.org/wiki/Timeline_of_antisemitism_in_the_20th_century#cite_note-118
720. https://en.wikipedia.org/wiki/1970s_Soviet_Union_aliyah
721. https://en.wikipedia.org/wiki/Southern_Baptist_Convention
722. https://en.wikipedia.org/wiki/Timeline_of_antisemitism_in_the_20th_century#cite_note-119
723. https://en.wikipedia.org/wiki/International_Catholic-Jewish_Liaison_Committee
724. https://en.wikipedia.org/wiki/Mordecai_Waxman
725. https://en.wikipedia.org/wiki/Magisterium
726. https://en.wikipedia.org/wiki/Southern_Baptist_Convention

"Therefore, be it RESOLVED, That this Convention go on record as opposed to any and all forms of anti-Semitism; that it declare anti-Semitism unchristian; that we messengers to this Convention pledge ourselves to combat anti-Semitism in every honorable, Christian way."

"Be it further RESOLVED, That Southern Baptists covenant to work positively to replace all anti-Semitic bias with the Christian attitude and practice of love for Jews, who along with all other men, are equally beloved of God."[120][727]

1972

11 Israeli Olympic athletes are taken hostage and eventually tortured and killed in the **Munich massacre**[728].

1974

Four Jewish girls were raped, murdered and mutilated after attempting to flee to Israel. Their bodies were discovered by border police in a cave in the **Zabdani Mountains**[729] northwest of Damascus along with the remains of two Jewish boys, Natan Shaya 18 and Kassem Abadi 20, victims of an earlier massacre.[121][730] Syrian authorities deposited the bodies of all six in sacks before the homes of their parents in the Jewish ghetto in Damascus.[122][731]

---

727. https://en.wikipedia.org/wiki/Timeline_of_antisemitism_in_the_20th_century#cite_note-120

728. https://en.wikipedia.org/wiki/Munich_massacre

729. https://en.wikipedia.org/wiki/Al-Zabadani

730. https://en.wikipedia.org/wiki/Timeline_of_antisemitism_in_the_20th_century#cite_note-121

731. https://en.wikipedia.org/wiki/Timeline_of_antisemitism_in_the_20th_century#cite_note-122

1974

Did Six Million Really Die?[732] *The Truth at Last*[123][733] is a Holocaust denial pamphlet allegedly written by British **National Front**[734] member **Richard Verrall**[735] under the pseudonym *Richard E. Harwood* and published by **Ernst Zündel**[736] in 1974.

1975

The United Nations passed a resolution determining that "Zionism is a form of racism and racial discrimination." (It was revoked in 1991, as mentioned below.)

1976

Arthur Butz[737]'s ***The Hoax of the Twentieth Century***[738]*: The case against the presumed extermination of European Jewry* was published.

1977

David Irving[739]'s Holocaust denying book ***Hitler's War***[740] was published.[124][741]

1977 March 9–11

1977 Washington, D.C. attack and hostage taking[742].

---

732. *https://en.wikipedia.org/wiki/Did_Six_Million_Really_Die%3F*

733. https://en.wikipedia.org/wiki/Timeline_of_antisemitism_in_the_20th_century#cite_note-123

734. https://en.wikipedia.org/wiki/National_Front_(UK)

735. https://en.wikipedia.org/wiki/Richard_Verrall_(political_writer)

736. https://en.wikipedia.org/wiki/Ernst_Z%C3%BCndel

737. https://en.wikipedia.org/wiki/Arthur_Butz

738. *https://en.wikipedia.org/wiki/The_Hoax_of_the_Twentieth_Century*

739. https://en.wikipedia.org/wiki/David_Irving

740. *https://en.wikipedia.org/wiki/Hitler%27s_War*

741. https://en.wikipedia.org/wiki/Timeline_of_antisemitism_in_the_20th_century#cite_note-124

1977 October 3

In suburban **St. Louis, Missouri**[743], **Joseph Paul Franklin**[744] hid in the bushes near a **Shaare Zedek Synagogue (University City, Missouri)**[745] and fired on a group attending services. In this incident, Franklin killed forty-two-year-old Gerald Gordon and wounded Steven Goldman and William Ash.

1977

In a 1977 *Globe-Democrat* column discussing **John Toland**[746]'s biography of **Adolf Hitler**[747], **Pat Buchanan**[748] wrote:

Though Hitler was indeed racist and anti-Semitic to the core, a man who without compunction could commit murder and genocide, he was also an individual of great courage, a soldier's soldier in the Great War, a political organizer of the first rank, a leader steeped in the history of Europe, who possessed oratorical powers that could awe even those who despised him... Hitler's success was not based on his extraordinary gifts alone. His genius was an intuitive sense of the mushiness, the character flaws, the weakness masquerading as morality that was in the hearts of the statesmen who stood in his path.[125][749]

Buchanan supporters say the paragraph is taken out of context.[126][750] They point out that in the same review Buchanan

742. https://en.wikipedia.org/wiki/1977_Washington,_D.C._attack_and_hostage_taking

743. https://en.wikipedia.org/wiki/St._Louis,_Missouri

744. https://en.wikipedia.org/wiki/Joseph_Paul_Franklin

745. https://en.wikipedia.org/wiki/Shaare_Zedek_Synagogue_(University_City,_Missouri)

746. https://en.wikipedia.org/wiki/John_Toland_(author)

747. https://en.wikipedia.org/wiki/Adolf_Hitler

748. https://en.wikipedia.org/wiki/Pat_Buchanan

749. https://en.wikipedia.org/wiki/Timeline_of_antisemitism_in_the_20th_century#cite_note-hitler-125

praised **Winston Churchill**[751] for seeing that "Hitler was marching along the road toward a New Order where Western civilization would not survive" and concluded that modern-day statesmen were not following that example.[125][752]

1977

National Socialist Party of America v. Village of Skokie[753], **432 U.S. 43**[754] (1977) (also known as ***Smith v. Collin***[755]; sometimes referred to as the **Skokie Affair**[756]), was a **United States Supreme Court**[757] case dealing with **freedom of assembly**[758]. The outcome was that the Illinois Supreme Court ruled that the use of the **swastika**[759] is a symbolic form of free speech entitled to **First Amendment**[760] protections and determined that the swastika itself did not constitute

---

750. **https://en.wikipedia.org/wiki/Timeline_of_antisemitism_in_the_20th_century#cite_note-nizkor-126**
751. **https://en.wikipedia.org/wiki/Winston_Churchill**
752. **https://en.wikipedia.org/wiki/Timeline_of_antisemitism_in_the_20th_century#cite_note-hitler-125**
753. ***https://en.wikipedia.org/wiki/National_Socialist_Party_of_America_v._Village_of_Skokie***
754. **https://en.wikipedia.org/wiki/Case_citation**
755. ***https://en.wikipedia.org/wiki/Smith_v._Collin***
756. **https://en.wikipedia.org/wiki/Skokie_Affair**
757. **https://en.wikipedia.org/wiki/Supreme_Court_of_the_United_States**
758. **https://en.wikipedia.org/wiki/Freedom_of_assembly**
759. **https://en.wikipedia.org/wiki/Swastika**
760. **https://en.wikipedia.org/wiki/First_Amendment_to_the_United_States_Constitution**

"**fighting words**[761]." Its ruling allowed the National Socialist Party of America to march.[127][762]

1978

In 1978 **Willis Carto**[763] founded the **Institute for Historical Review**[764] (IHR), an organization dedicated to publicly challenging the commonly accepted history of the Holocaust.[128][765]

1978/1979

In December 1978 and January 1979, **Robert Faurisson**[766], a French professor of literature at the **University of Lyon**[767], wrote two letters to ***Le Monde***[768] claiming that the **gas chambers**[769] used by the Nazis to exterminate the Jews did not exist.

1979

A House Joint resolution 1014 designated 28 and 29 April 1979 as "**The Days of Remembrance of the Victims of the Holocaust (DRVH)**[770]." After that the Days of Remembrance of the Victims of

---

761. https://en.wikipedia.org/wiki/Fighting_words
762. https://en.wikipedia.org/wiki/Timeline_of_antisemitism_in_the_20th_century#cite_note-caselaw.lp.findlaw.com-127
763. https://en.wikipedia.org/wiki/Willis_Carto
764. https://en.wikipedia.org/wiki/Institute_for_Historical_Review
765. https://en.wikipedia.org/wiki/Timeline_of_antisemitism_in_the_20th_century#cite_note-128
766. https://en.wikipedia.org/wiki/Robert_Faurisson
767. https://en.wikipedia.org/wiki/University_of_Lyon
768. *https://en.wikipedia.org/wiki/Le_Monde*
769. https://en.wikipedia.org/wiki/Gas_chambers
770. https://en.wikipedia.org/wiki/The_Days_of_Remembrance_of_the_Victims_of_the_Holocaust_(DRVH)

the Holocaust (DRVH) has been an annual 8-day period designated by the United States Congress for civic commemorations and special educational programs that help citizens remember and draw lessons from the Holocaust.

1979

When the **Anti-Defamation League**[771] accused **Lyndon LaRouche**[772] of antisemitism in 1979, he filed a $26-million libel suit; however, the case failed when Justice Michael Dontzin of the New York Supreme Court ruled that it was **fair comment**[773], and that the facts "reasonably give rise" to that description.[129][774][130][775]

1979

"Jewish Princess" is a song by **Frank Zappa**[776] released on his album ***Sheik Yerbouti***[777] in 1979. The song is a humorous look at the **Jewish-American princess stereotype**[778] which attracted attention from the **Anti-Defamation League**[779], to which Zappa denied an

---

771. https://en.wikipedia.org/wiki/Anti-Defamation_League
772. https://en.wikipedia.org/wiki/Lyndon_LaRouche
773. https://en.wikipedia.org/wiki/Fair_comment
774. https://en.wikipedia.org/wiki/Timeline_of_antisemitism_in_the_20th_century#cite_note 129
775. https://en.wikipedia.org/wiki/Timeline_of_antisemitism_in_the_20th_century#cite_note-130
776. https://en.wikipedia.org/wiki/Frank_Zappa
777. *https://en.wikipedia.org/wiki/Sheik_Yerbouti*
778. https://en.wikipedia.org/wiki/Jewish-American_princess_stereotype
779. https://en.wikipedia.org/wiki/Anti-Defamation_League

apology, arguing: "Unlike the unicorn, such creatures do exist – and deserve to be 'commemorated' with their own special opus". In an interview with **Spin**[780] magazine he was almost offended saying, "...as if to say there is no such thing as a Jewish Princess. Like I invented this?"[131][781] Biographer Barry Miles claimed in his book, *Frank Zappa* (Atlantic Books of London, 2005), that the ADL asked the Federal Communications Commission (FCC) to ban the record from being played on the air – a symbolic effort given that the song was not being played anyway.

1980s[edit[782]]

1980, 27 July

1980 Antwerp attack[783].[132][784][133][785]

780. https://en.wikipedia.org/wiki/Spin_(magazine)

781. https://en.wikipedia.org/wiki/Timeline_of_antisemitism_in_the_20th_century#cite_note-LLC1991-131

782. https://en.wikipedia.org/w/index.php?title=Timeline_of_antisemitism_in_the_20th_century&action=edit§ion=9

783. https://en.wikipedia.org/wiki/1980_Antwerp_attack

784. https://en.wikipedia.org/wiki/Timeline_of_antisemitism_in_the_20th_century#cite_note-GlobeYouthDies-132

785. https://en.wikipedia.org/wiki/Timeline_of_antisemitism_in_the_20th_century#cite_note-WaPoAttack-133

1980, 3 October

1980 Paris synagogue bombing[786].[134][787][135][788][136][789][137][790]

1980

In 1980, the **Institute for Historical Review**[791] promised a $50,000 reward to anyone who could prove that Jews were gassed at Auschwitz. **Mel Mermelstein**[792] wrote a **letter to the editors**[793] of the ***LA Times***[794] and others including ***The Jerusalem Post***[795]. The IHR wrote back, offering him $50,000 for proof that Jews were, in fact, gassed in the gas chambers at Auschwitz. Mermelstein, in turn,

---

786. https://en.wikipedia.org/wiki/1980_Paris_synagogue_bombing

787. https://en.wikipedia.org/wiki/Timeline_of_antisemitism_in_the_20th_century#cite_note-JewishTargets-134

788. https://en.wikipedia.org/wiki/Timeline_of_antisemitism_in_the_20th_century#cite_note-lemonde.fr-135

789. https://en.wikipedia.org/wiki/Timeline_of_antisemitism_in_the_20th_century#cite_note-136

790. https://en.wikipedia.org/wiki/Timeline_of_antisemitism_in_the_20th_century#cite_note-137

791. https://en.wikipedia.org/wiki/Institute_for_Historical_Review

792. https://en.wikipedia.org/wiki/Mel_Mermelstein

793. https://en.wikipedia.org/wiki/Letter_to_the_editor

794. *https://en.wikipedia.org/wiki/LA_Times*

795. *https://en.wikipedia.org/wiki/The_Jerusalem_Post*

submitted a notarized account of his internment at Auschwitz and how he witnessed Nazi guards ushering his mother and two sisters and others towards (as he learned later) gas chamber number five. Despite this, the IHR refused to pay the reward. Represented by public interest attorney **William John Cox**[796], Mermelstein subsequently sued the IHR in the **Superior Court of Los Angeles County**[797]M for **breach of contract**[798], **anticipatory repudiation**[799], **libel**[800], **injurious denial of established fact**[801], **intentional infliction of emotional distress**[802], and **declaratory relief**[803] (see **case no. C 356 542**[804]). On 9 October 1981, both parties in the Mermelstein case filed motions for **summary judgment**[805] in consideration of which Judge Thomas T. Johnson of the **Superior Court of Los Angeles County**[806] took "**judicial notice**[807] of the fact that Jews were gassed to death at the Auschwitz Concentration Camp in Poland during the summer of

796. https://en.wikipedia.org/wiki/William_John_Cox

797. https://en.wikipedia.org/wiki/Superior_Court_of_Los_Angeles_County

798. https://en.wikipedia.org/wiki/Breach_of_contract

799. https://en.wikipedia.org/wiki/Anticipatory_repudiation

800. https://en.wikipedia.org/wiki/Libel

801. https://en.wikipedia.org/wiki/Injurious_denial_of_established_fact

802. https://en.wikipedia.org/wiki/Intentional_infliction_of_emotional_distress

803. https://en.wikipedia.org/wiki/Declaratory_relief

804. https://en.wikipedia.org/w/
index.php?title=Case_no._C_356_542&action=edit&redlink=1

805. https://en.wikipedia.org/wiki/Summary_judgment

806. https://en.wikipedia.org/wiki/Superior_Court_of_Los_Angeles_County

807. https://en.wikipedia.org/wiki/Judicial_notice

1944,"[138][808][139][809] judicial notice meaning that the court treated the gas chambers as common knowledge, and therefore did not require evidence that the gas chambers existed. On 5 August 1985, Judge Robert A. Wenke entered a judgment based upon the **Stipulation**[810] for Entry of Judgment agreed upon by the parties on 22 July 1985. The judgment required IHR and other defendants to pay $90,000 to Mermelstein and to issue a letter of apology to "Mr. Mel Mermelstein, a survivor of Auschwitz-Birkenau and Buchenwald, and all other survivors of Auschwitz" for "pain, anguish and suffering" caused to them.[139][811]

Early 1980s

Jesse Jackson[812] was criticized in the early 1980s for remarks made to a reporter where he referred to New York City as "Hymietown".[140][813][141][814] (**Hymie**[815] is a **pejorative**[816] term for Jews.) Jackson ultimately acknowledged he had used the term, and

---

808. https://en.wikipedia.org/wiki/Timeline_of_antisemitism_in_the_20th_century#cite_note-NYT-138
809. https://en.wikipedia.org/wiki/Timeline_of_antisemitism_in_the_20th_century#cite_note-order-139
810. https://en.wikipedia.org/wiki/Stipulation
811. https://en.wikipedia.org/wiki/Timeline_of_antisemitism_in_the_20th_century#cite_note-order-139
812. https://en.wikipedia.org/wiki/Jesse_Jackson
813. https://en.wikipedia.org/wiki/Timeline_of_antisemitism_in_the_20th_century#cite_note-aims-140

said he had been wrong; however, he also said that he had considered the conversation with the reporter to be off-the-record at the time he made the remarks.[141][817] Jackson apologized during a speech before national Jewish leaders in a **Manchester, New Hampshire**[818] synagogue, but an enduring split between Jackson and many in the Jewish community continued at least through the 1990s.[141][819]

1981 August 29

1981 Vienna synagogue attack[820].[142][821][143][822][144][823]

---

814. https://en.wikipedia.org/wiki/Timeline_of_antisemitism_in_the_20th_century#cite_note-wapo-141

815. https://en.wikipedia.org/wiki/List_of_ethnic_slurs_of_Jews

816. https://en.wikipedia.org/wiki/Pejorative

817. https://en.wikipedia.org/wiki/Timeline_of_antisemitism_in_the_20th_century#cite_note-wapo-141

818. https://en.wikipedia.org/wiki/Manchester,_New_Hampshire

819. https://en.wikipedia.org/wiki/Timeline_of_antisemitism_in_the_20th_century#cite_note-wapo-141

820. https://en.wikipedia.org/wiki/1981_Vienna_synagogue_attack

821. https://en.wikipedia.org/wiki/Timeline_of_antisemitism_in_the_20th_century#cite_note-142

822. https://en.wikipedia.org/wiki/Timeline_of_antisemitism_in_the_20th_century#cite_note-143

823. https://en.wikipedia.org/wiki/Timeline_of_antisemitism_in_the_20th_century#cite_note-query.nytimes.com-144

1981 October 20

1981 Antwerp synagogue bombing[824].[145][825]

1981

The **Southern Baptist Convention**[826] passed a "Resolution On Anti-Semitism" stating in part, "Be it therefore RESOLVED, That the messengers at the 1981 Southern Baptist Convention meeting in Los Angeles, June 9–11, 1981, commend our Southern Baptist Convention leaders as they seek sincere friendship and meaningful dialogue with our Jewish neighbors."[146][827]

1981

Elana Steinberg was killed by her husband Steven Steinberg, who claimed that she was a "spoiled, over-indulged brat – the stereotypical **Jewish American Princess**[828]," and that she made him insane by spending and insisting that he become more successful; he was found not guilty.[147][829]

1981-3

---

824. https://en.wikipedia.org/wiki/1981_Antwerp_synagogue_bombing

825. https://en.wikipedia.org/wiki/Timeline_of_antisemitism_in_the_20th_century#cite_note-145

826. https://en.wikipedia.org/wiki/Southern_Baptist_Convention

827. https://en.wikipedia.org/wiki/Timeline_of_antisemitism_in_the_20th_century#cite_note-146

828. https://en.wikipedia.org/wiki/Jewish_American_Princess

From 1981 to 1982, Holocaust denier **Ernst Zündel**[830] had his mailing privileges suspended by the Canadian government on the grounds that he had been using the mail to send **hate propaganda**[831], a criminal offence in Canada. Zündel then began shipping from a post office box in **Niagara Falls, New York**[832], until the ban on his mailing in Canada was lifted in January 1983.

1982

A bomb placed by neo-Nazis exploded outside the Jewish hunter of Nazis **Simon Wiesenthal**[833]'s house in Vienna on 11 June 1982, after which police guards were stationed outside his home 24 hours a day.[148][834][149][835]

1982 October 9

Great Synagogue of Rome attack[836] takes place.

1982

829. https://en.wikipedia.org/wiki/Timeline_of_antisemitism_in_the_20th_century#cite_note-147
830. https://en.wikipedia.org/wiki/Ernst_Z%C3%BCndel
831. https://en.wikipedia.org/wiki/Hate_speech
832. https://en.wikipedia.org/wiki/Niagara_Falls,_New_York
833. https://en.wikipedia.org/wiki/Simon_Wiesenthal
834. https://en.wikipedia.org/wiki/Timeline_of_antisemitism_in_the_20th_century#cite_note-148
835. https://en.wikipedia.org/wiki/Timeline_of_antisemitism_in_the_20th_century#cite_note-149
836. https://en.wikipedia.org/wiki/Great_Synagogue_of_Rome_attack

The thesis of the 1982 doctoral dissertation of **Mahmoud Abbas**[837], a co-founder of **Fatah**[838] and president of the **Palestinian National Authority**[839], was "The Secret Connection between the Nazis and the Leaders of the Zionist Movement".**[150]**[840]**[151]**[841]**[152]**[842] In his 1983 book ***The Other Side: the Secret Relationship Between Nazism and Zionism***[843] based on the dissertation, Abbas denied that six million Jews had been murdered in the Holocaust; dismissing it as a "myth" and a "fantastic lie".**[153]**[844] At most, he wrote, 890,000 Jews were killed by the Germans. Abbas claimed that the number of deaths has been exaggerated for political purposes. "It seems that the interest of the Zionist movement, however, is to inflate this figure [of Holocaust deaths] so that their gains will be greater. This led them to emphasize this figure [six million] in order to gain the solidarity of international public opinion with Zionism. Many scholars have

837. https://en.wikipedia.org/wiki/Mahmoud_Abbas

838. https://en.wikipedia.org/wiki/Fatah

839. https://en.wikipedia.org/wiki/Palestinian_National_Authority

840. https://en.wikipedia.org/wiki/Timeline_of_antisemitism_in_the_20th_century#cite_note-150

841. https://en.wikipedia.org/wiki/Timeline_of_antisemitism_in_the_20th_century#cite_note-151

842. https://en.wikipedia.org/wiki/Timeline_of_antisemitism_in_the_20th_century#cite_note-wiesenthal-152

843. *https://en.wikipedia.org/wiki/The_Other_Side:_the_Secret_Relationship_Between_Nazism_and_Zionism*

844. https://en.wikipedia.org/wiki/Timeline_of_antisemitism_in_the_20th_century#cite_note-Abbas-153

debated the figure of six million and reached stunning conclusions—fixing the number of Jewish victims at only a few hundred thousand."[152][845][154][846][155][847][156][848][157][849] In his March 2006 interview with ***Haaretz***[850], Abbas stated, "I wrote in detail about the Holocaust and said I did not want to discuss numbers. I quoted an argument between historians in which various numbers of casualties were mentioned. One wrote there were 12 million victims and another wrote there were 800,000. I have no desire to argue with the figures. The Holocaust was a terrible, unforgivable crime against the Jewish nation, a crime against humanity that cannot be accepted by humankind. The Holocaust was a terrible thing and nobody can claim I denied it."[158][851] While acknowledging the existence of the

---

845. **https://en.wikipedia.org/wiki/Timeline_of_antisemitism_in_the_20th_century#cite_note-wiesenthal-152**

846. **https://en.wikipedia.org/wiki/Timeline_of_antisemitism_in_the_20th_century#cite_note-wymaninstitute.org-154**

847. **https://en.wikipedia.org/wiki/Timeline_of_antisemitism_in_the_20th_century#cite_note-tomgross-155**

848. **https://en.wikipedia.org/wiki/Timeline_of_antisemitism_in_the_20th_century#cite_note-156**

849. **https://en.wikipedia.org/wiki/Timeline_of_antisemitism_in_the_20th_century#cite_note-pmw-157**

850. ***https://en.wikipedia.org/wiki/Haaretz***

851. **https://en.wikipedia.org/wiki/Timeline_of_antisemitism_in_the_20th_century#cite_note-158**

Holocaust in 2006 and 2014,[159][852] Abbas has defended the position that Zionists collaborated with the Nazis to perpetrate it. In 2012, Abbas told **Al Mayadeen**[853], a Beirut TV station affiliated with Iran and Hezbollah, that he "challenges anyone who can deny that the Zionist movement had ties with the Nazis before World War II".[160][854]

1982 September 18

Great Synagogue of Europe[855] attacked by a man with a submachine gun, seriously wounding four people.[161][856][162][857] The attack has been attributed to the **Abu Nidal Organization**[858].[163][859]

1982

852. https://en.wikipedia.org/wiki/Timeline_of_antisemitism_in_the_20th_century#cite_note-Heinous-159
853. https://en.wikipedia.org/wiki/Al_Mayadeen
854. https://en.wikipedia.org/wiki/Timeline_of_antisemitism_in_the_20th_century#cite_note-Link-160
855. https://en.wikipedia.org/wiki/Great_Synagogue_of_Europe
856. https://en.wikipedia.org/wiki/Timeline_of_antisemitism_in_the_20th_century#cite_note-161
857. https://en.wikipedia.org/wiki/Timeline_of_antisemitism_in_the_20th_century#cite_note-162
858. https://en.wikipedia.org/wiki/Abu_Nidal_Organization
859. https://en.wikipedia.org/wiki/Timeline_of_antisemitism_in_the_20th_century#cite_note-163

In the book ***Against Sadomasochism***[860], **Susan Leigh Star**[861] criticizes the use of **swastikas**[862] and other **Nazi**[863] imagery by some BDSM practitioners as anti-Semitic and racist.[164][864]

1983

The **Lutheran Church–Missouri Synod**[865] officially disassociates itself from "intemperate remarks about Jews" in Luther's works. Since then, many **Lutheran church**[866] bodies and organizations have issued similar statements. (See **Martin Luther and the Jews**[867])

1984

On the evening of 18 June 1984, **Alan Berg**[868] was fatally shot in the driveway of his Denver home by members of the **white nationalist**[869] group **The Order**[870]. His provocative talk show sought to flush out "the anti-Semitism latent in the area's conservative population". He succeeded in provoking members of The Order to

860. *https://en.wikipedia.org/wiki/Against_Sadomasochism*

861. https://en.wikipedia.org/wiki/Susan_Leigh_Star

862. https://en.wikipedia.org/wiki/Swastikas

863. https://en.wikipedia.org/wiki/Nazi

864. https://en.wikipedia.org/wiki/Timeline_of_antisemitism_in_the_20th_century#cite note-164

865. https://en.wikipedia.org/wiki/Lutheran_Church%E2%80%93Missouri_Synod

866. https://en.wikipedia.org/wiki/Lutheran_church

867. https://en.wikipedia.org/wiki/Martin_Luther_and_the_Jews

868. https://en.wikipedia.org/wiki/Alan_Berg

869. https://en.wikipedia.org/wiki/White_Nationalism

870. https://en.wikipedia.org/wiki/The_Order_(white_supremacist_group)

engage him in conversations on this talk show and his "often-abrasive on-air persona" ignited the anger of The Order.[165][871][166][872] Subsequently, members of The Order involved in the killing were identified as being part of a group planning to kill prominent Jews.[167][873] Ultimately, two members of The Order, **David Lane**[874] and Bruce Pierce, were convicted for their involvement in the case, though neither of **homicide**[875].

1984

In 1984, **James Keegstra**[876], a Canadian high-school teacher, was charged under the Canadian ***Criminal Code***[877] for "promoting hatred against an identifiable group by communicating anti-Semitic statements to his students". During class, he would describe Jews as a people of profound evil who had "created the Holocaust to gain sympathy." He also tested his students in exams on his theories and opinion of Jews.

Keegstra was charged under s 281.2(2) of the *Criminal Code* (now s 319(2), which provides that "Every one who, by communicating

871. https://en.wikipedia.org/wiki/Timeline_of_antisemitism_in_the_20th_century#cite_note-denverpost-165
872. https://en.wikipedia.org/wiki/Timeline_of_antisemitism_in_the_20th_century#cite_note-ChiTrib-166
873. https://en.wikipedia.org/wiki/Timeline_of_antisemitism_in_the_20th_century#cite_note-167
874. https://en.wikipedia.org/wiki/David_Lane_(white_nationalist)
875. https://en.wikipedia.org/wiki/Homicide
876. https://en.wikipedia.org/wiki/James_Keegstra
877. *https://en.wikipedia.org/wiki/Criminal_Code_(Canada)*

statements, other than in private conversation, wilfully promotes hatred against any identifiable group" commits a criminal offence.[168][878] He was convicted at trial before the **Alberta Court of Queen's Bench**[879]. The court rejected the argument, advanced by Keegstra and his lawyer, **Doug Christie**[880], that promoting hatred is a constitutionally protected freedom of expression as per **s 2(b) of the Canadian Charter of Rights and Freedoms**[881]. Keegstra appealed to the **Alberta Court of Appeal**[882]. That court agreed with Keegstra, and he was acquitted. The Crown then appealed the case to the **Supreme Court of Canada**[883], which rule by a 4–3 majority that promoting hatred could be **justifiably**[884] restricted under **s 1 of the Charter**[885]. The Supreme Court restored Keegstra's conviction.[169][886] He was fired from his teaching position shortly afterwards.[170][887]

---

878. https://en.wikipedia.org/wiki/Timeline_of_antisemitism_in_the_20th_century#cite_note-168

879. https://en.wikipedia.org/wiki/Alberta_Court_of_Queen%27s_Bench

880. https://en.wikipedia.org/wiki/Doug_Christie_(lawyer)

881. https://en.wikipedia.org/wiki/Section_Two_of_the_Canadian_Charter_of_Rights_and_Freedoms

882. https://en.wikipedia.org/wiki/Alberta_Court_of_Appeal

883. https://en.wikipedia.org/wiki/Supreme_Court_of_Canada

884. https://en.wikipedia.org/wiki/R._v._Keegstra#Reasons_of_the_court

885. https://en.wikipedia.org/wiki/Section_1_of_the_canadian_charter_of_rights_and_freedoms

886. https://en.wikipedia.org/wiki/Timeline_of_antisemitism_in_the_20th_century#cite_note-169

1985, 22 July

1985 Copenhagen bombings[888].[171]889[172]890[173]891

1985

At a meeting of the Nation of Islam at **Madison Square Garden**[892] in 1985, **Louis Farrakhan**[893] said of the Jews: "And don't you forget, when it's God who puts you in the ovens, it's forever!"[174]894

1985

On 24 December 1985, **David Lewis Rice**[895], a follower of the right-wing extremist group the **Duck Club**[896], gained entry to the

887. https://en.wikipedia.org/wiki/Timeline_of_antisemitism_in_the_20th_century#cite_note-170

888. https://en.wikipedia.org/wiki/1985_Copenhagen_bombings

889. https://en.wikipedia.org/wiki/Timeline_of_antisemitism_in_the_20th_century#cite_note-TV2April2008-171

890. https://en.wikipedia.org/wiki/Timeline_of_antisemitism_in_the_20th_century#cite_note-172

891. https://en.wikipedia.org/wiki/Timeline_of_antisemitism_in_the_20th_century#cite_note-TerroristExplosions-173

892. https://en.wikipedia.org/wiki/Madison_Square_Garden

893. https://en.wikipedia.org/wiki/Louis_Farrakhan

894. https://en.wikipedia.org/wiki/Timeline_of_antisemitism_in_the_20th_century#cite_note-174

Seattle[897] home of **civil litigation**[898][175][899][176][900] attorney Charles Goldmark using a toy gun and pretending to be a deliveryman.[177][901] He tied the family up, **chloroformed**[902] them into unconsciousness, beat them with a steam iron, and stabbed them.[177][903] Rice mistakenly believed the family to be Jewish and **Communist**[904].[178][905] In 1998, he **pleaded guilty**[906] to the crimes[179][907] in exchange for avoiding the death penalty. The

895. https://en.wikipedia.org/wiki/David_Lewis_Rice

896. https://en.wikipedia.org/wiki/Duck_Club

897. https://en.wikipedia.org/wiki/Seattle

898. https://en.wikipedia.org/wiki/Civil_litigation

899. https://en.wikipedia.org/wiki/Timeline_of_antisemitism_in_the_20th_century#cite_note-175

900. https://en.wikipedia.org/wiki/Timeline_of_antisemitism_in_the_20th_century#cite_note-HistoryLink-176

901. https://en.wikipedia.org/wiki/Timeline_of_antisemitism_in_the_20th_century#cite_note-EDR-177

902. https://en.wikipedia.org/wiki/Chloroformed

903. https://en.wikipedia.org/wiki/Timeline_of_antisemitism_in_the_20th_century#cite_note-EDR-177

904. https://en.wikipedia.org/wiki/Communist

905. https://en.wikipedia.org/wiki/Timeline_of_antisemitism_in_the_20th_century#cite_note-178

906. https://en.wikipedia.org/wiki/Guilty_plea

907. https://en.wikipedia.org/wiki/Timeline_of_antisemitism_in_the_20th_century#cite_note-179

Goldmark Murders remain one of the most notorious antisemitic hate crimes as well as **politically motivated killings**[908] in recent memory in the United States, even though the victims were not actually Jewish and Communist as the killer mistakenly believed.

Ronald Reagan[909] visited a German military cemetery in **Bitburg**[910] to lay a wreath with West German Chancellor **Helmut Kohl**[911]. It was determined that the cemetery held the graves of forty-nine members of the **Waffen-SS**[912]. Reagan issued a statement that called the Nazi soldiers buried in that cemetery as themselves "victims," a designation which ignited a stir over whether Reagan had equated the SS men to victims of **the Holocaust**[913]; **Pat Buchanan**[914], Reagan's Director of Communications, argued that the president did not equate the SS members with the actual Holocaust.[180][915] Now strongly urged to cancel the visit,[181][916] the president responded that it would be wrong to back down on a promise he had made to

908. https://en.wikipedia.org/wiki/Right-wing_violence

909. https://en.wikipedia.org/wiki/Ronald_Reagan

910. https://en.wikipedia.org/wiki/Bitburg

911. https://en.wikipedia.org/wiki/Helmut_Kohl

912. https://en.wikipedia.org/wiki/Waffen-SS

913. https://en.wikipedia.org/wiki/The_Holocaust

914. https://en.wikipedia.org/wiki/Pat_Buchanan

915. https://en.wikipedia.org/wiki/Timeline_of_antisemitism_in_the_20th_century#cite_note-180

916. https://en.wikipedia.org/wiki/Timeline_of_antisemitism_in_the_20th_century#cite_note-181

Chancellor Kohl. He ultimately attended the ceremony where two military generals laid a wreath.[182][917]

917. https://en.wikipedia.org/wiki/Timeline_of_antisemitism_in_the_20th_century#cite_note-182

www.ingramcontent.com/pod-product-compliance
Ingram Content Group UK Ltd.
Pitfield, Milton Keynes, MK11 3LW, UK
UKHW021659190726
13853UKWH00001B/355

9 798224 920839